The Long Road Home

Dear Wendy,
"Que Sera Sera"
Whatever will be will be"

Joann B. Namorato

The Long Road Home

Memories of September 11th

Joann B. Namorato

Writers Advantage
New York   Lincoln   Shanghai

The Long Road Home
Memories of September 11th

Writers Advantage
an imprint of iUniverse, Inc.

For information address:
iUniverse
2021 Pine Lake Road, Suite 100
Lincoln, NE 68512
www.iuniverse.com

ISBN: 0-595-24676-1

Printed in the United States of America

Contents

The Poems That Healed My Heart

In Memory of Mark Petrocelli and Brian Cannizzaro

MY UNSUNG HEROES of SEPTEMBER 11th, 2001

Nothing will ever compare to the loss of your lives, but I hope by enlightening people to the events of that horrific day we can all learn to live in a world together without differences.

Dedicated to my family and friends for giving back to me the strength I believed was gone forever.

To Dr. Seddio, my psychologist: You shared in my tears and pain, and you were right, I have made it back 95 %.

Finally to McMahon, Martine & Gallagher, you held me in the palm of your hands.

GOD DOES HAVE ANGELS HERE ON EARTH

HEARTFELT THANKS TO MOUNT LORETTO, CATHOLIC CHARITIES, SAFE HORIZON, MICHAEL DIMAGGIO, STEVEN RYNN, AND DR. CARDELLO

Chapter One

My Return To New York

The morning was dark and frightening, just the noise of heavy equipment off in the distance near Ground Zero. The overhead skies, once bright each morning, were now overshadowed by gray smoke and the everlasting evil of the prior three weeks. When I finally reached the security check-in, and after identifying whom I was and where I worked, I was escorted by a young female police officer to my office building. With every step, I felt scared and unsure if I could manage to walk so close to the memories of that nightmare that still echoed in my heart. The nightmarish dream continues to awake me from a deep sleep and keeps reminding me that September 11th was a reality. As I walked slowly past the debris, I recalled the horror of the screaming people as they ran toward Broadway to escape the fear and apparent death that currently were knocking on their door. There is no doubt it will always remain the worst day in the lives of many Americans. I found myself stepping over pipes, debris and burned tree branches only to find a padlock with chains blocking what once was the entrance to the office where I worked. A handwritten sign on the wood frame informed both the officer and I that the building would open at eight a.m. I suppose my employer forgot to mention the change to me considering my regular scheduled hours, since I had begun working there, were six a.m. to three p.m. I was anxious while thinking about how I needed to wait for almost two hours in the environment that stood before me. I was told by the young officer to return to security and someone would come for me when the maintenance crew arrived to open the building. In the meanwhile, I stood gazing out at Ground Zero from Fulton Street and Broadway. The noise, the smell and the crowds photographing the horror were all prevalent factors, and I was just hoping to find solace in all this misery. People were staring down at the site, the front part of one building just standing as a symbol of what took place just a few weeks earlier. I could not look at it, so I turned my head toward City Hall and began to think about the unforgettable day that brought our nation to our knees. I could feel the agitation building in me as I began to cry for those who did not make it out on September 11th. Here it was October 3rd and I shuttered at the thought of going through this procedure each day just to keep my life in some kind of order. Fortunately for me, the building attendant arrived at seven-fifteen a.m. and I was able to once again walk down Vesey Street and into the building which had been my second home since 1998. The outside facade of the building was covered in gray ash while metal pieces and piles of office paper captured during the collapse of the towers were stacked against the building. I no longer thought that these doors leading to my office would ever be a safe-haven again. Upon arriving at my job that morning I had the task of unloading all the computers, files and mail which I had helped move the prior day from our temporary office in Sheepshead Bay, Brooklyn, after the attack.

I was born in the South Bronx, grew up there until I was eleven and after both my parents passed away, I was moved to an orphanage in Staten Island where I remained until I was seventeen. I wonder how I have made it from then until now. In my heart, I knew my bosses relied on my dedication. I was never sick, never late, always there, and always ready. This was now going to be different. I looked at my office, still covered in ash with a smell that I have never been able to describe to anyone. Maybe because it was a new smell, something that was frightening, the smell of death and of a new type of war. As the morning wore on, I tried to block out my feelings. I continued to connect the computers and unpack the sixteen boxes. At around ten a.m., I approached my one boss who actually seemed concerned about the way I was feeling when he arrived at the office that morning. I felt so peculiar being in the area considering the asbestos, the noise, the cranes and the removal of the bodies and body parts. I told him how I was slowly beginning to unravel just being in the vicinity. He told me they were looking at space in midtown Manhattan and were hoping to move within the next six months. Unfortunately, that was not the answer I had anticipated and I expressed my displeasure of the here and now. The other employees had returned a few days earlier, I could see they were already used to all the commotion and had I been given a chance maybe I could have been more relaxed in the following days. I received a call from one of them telling me that she would not be in because she was tired and I wondered why I had even showed up. I pondered whether she was really tired or just scared since a day earlier she said she was going to look for a job closer to home. I guess that was until she was offered my position, after I was relieved of my duties because of my continued stress and anxiety.

At lunch, I decided to take a two-block walk to Modell's Sporting Store on Broadway and Fulton Street to purchase tee-shirts, knowing that the profits would be donated to the now-established World Trade Center Fund. I thought maybe if I took a walk, I might feel a little less uneasy about being closed in at the office. As I stepped out of the building, I fell over boards still cluttering the streets a few hundred feet from where Tower One once stood. I landed on my ankle and against a piece of metal when a man dressed in army fatigues helped me to my feet. I realized at that point that I did not want to be out in the area and wanted immediately to return to the office. As I approached the security check-in, I was told I would have to get back on line despite the fact that I had been through earlier. At the tender age of fifty, I had been experiencing Irritable

Bowel Syndrome for the past year and with all that was going on I had forgotten to take my medication, which I took each day at nine in the morning. The security wait was approximately fifteen minutes, fifteen minutes that I did not have and so now I truly was agitated and quite embarrassed of my present situation. Upon finally passing through security I ran into one of the bosses of the company who told me how his wife wanted to come downtown, but he had demanded she stay away from all the commotion and panic, which I went through during that unforgettable Tuesday morning. Why was I putting myself through this situation so soon after the shock of losing friends in the collapse? Why couldn't we have just stayed in Brooklyn a few more weeks? None of my bosses were there that frightful day. So how could they ever comprehend what I had been through? I heard the plane cut its engines over my head and I had seen both planes crash and watching helplessly as people jumped to their deaths. I still wonder how desperate they must have felt that they would rather choose to take the leap of faith. I remember watching in horror as the fire and smoke blazed through the towers and I recall my urgency to escape. While at the office I felt as if I was working in a cemetery, for at that time very few bodies had been recovered. The pain of seeing so many of the families crying on and about Broadway was the most heart-wrenching reminder I had of the tragedy.

The events leading up to September 11th have been told over and over in different forms, stories and nonstop memorials. I was one of the working-class of lower Manhattan and I need to tell you the pain from not just that day, but for the past eleven months

I had worked on Staten Island for many years. When I was preparing to send two children off to college, I realized the expenses that I was about to incur realistically could not be earned by the salary I made in my hometown. At that time I decided it was time to go back into Manhattan. I was a paralegal and the law firms in the downtown area were numerous. Unfortunately, as it turned out, I selected the wrong one of the four from which I had been offered. Even back then in 1998, I had many reservations about working near the World Trade Center because of the prior bombing in 1993. During that time, I only watched on TV the horror and pain of those people who frantically tried to escape. I discussed this situation with many friends and family, which brought about the observation that no one would ever bomb the same place a second time. How about a third time? Inside, I had a premonition that a terrorist act would happen again, but I never really know when my premonitions are going to be on target. My life changed so dramatically after taking the job on Vesey Street. The glamour of working in New York engulfed me, considering it had been nearly twenty-five years since I worked over on Broad Street for a shipping firm and as a teller for Banker's Trust on Wall Street. Downtown offered shopping, people and the opportunity of meeting and working with a new company. Although I can usually sense good character traits, I do admit my judgment was not at its best when going to this particular firm. My dedication and desire to be a success has overshadowed my life in so many ways for me on that day. At my prior jobs just like this one, I had always given my best, always gave 110% of myself. I guess that proves that no matter how much you give, they always want a little more. When I began my new adventure across from the World Trade Center, I promised myself I would be strong and that only God would truly be able to protect me during any trials I might face. I took this firm, which was totally disorganized and way behind in their workload and brought them to a new plateau as an organization. I put all my fears behind me and began a challenging position as a New York City paralegal in the heart of the financial district. Would this be a decision I would come to regret or would it make me stronger in the long run? I never realized the decision I chose years ago would now put me into regular therapy and large doses of medication to relax my brain and heal my heart. Please allow me to begin to tell you my story from the beginning. Please understand that I have never written a book, but I hope that the words will come to me as I tell you the horror that one woman faced that memorable day of September 11th, 2001.

Chapter Two

Back To The Beginning

I was born in the South Bronx of New York City in 1950, the child of an alcoholic mother and a merchant marine father. My father was rarely home except for holidays. I grew up in a tenement with many friends and few family values. When my parents were together, which was rare, they fought and beat each other, causing the surrounding neighbors to shelter me many times. Daddy died in 1958 of an asthma attack. I do not remember seeing my mother cry. That has always been a memory that comes back to haunt me, as my life took its twists and turns. I think back to that eight-year-old stage, looking at their relationship and wondering, is this the way married people act? Sometimes when I watched television, I would see families like "Father Knows Best" and "I Love Lucy" and wondered why their relationships didn't include physical abuse. I guess that is why she didn't cry when he died. When I think back to those few child-hood memories, I know that my parents were as different as day and night. I went through life looking for someone to shelter me when the fighting became violent. I promised myself to find some happiness, some-where, someday. I was not surprised that in the end there were no tears. My mother became more of a drinker after his death. A few years later my older brother, John, at the tender age of twenty, was serving in the United States Navy. Unfortunately, he became involved with drugs and was beginning to lose his fight to overcome his addiction. I never truly understood it until later in life, but I never did forget finding him slumped over the bathroom toilet and telling Mom that Johnny was sick. I ran back downstairs to finish a game of skulls with the neighborhood kids. As the game continued, the sirens of an ambulance pulled up in front of our apartment complex, rushing to aid someone in the building. To the neighborhood kids, this was excitement as we followed wondering who was in need of their help. It was when they knocked on Apartment 3D that I realized that Johnny must be really sick if Mom had made a desperate call for help. After a few minutes, the ambulance attendants came out without a patient. Johnny was dead! He died of an overdose of heroin after just being released from rehabilitation. Little did I know at that moment that my life was going to change forever and my childhood was over. I believed in God at a very young age and knew he would not allow things to get any worse. I could not imagine seeing my brother laying there, knowing he was not coming back. What could be worst after seeing someone you loved and looked up to end his life on a toilet? I was about to be thrust into the world of uncertainty and the realization of becoming an adult at the tender age of ten. Sometimes I wondered which was worst, being a street kid in the corrupt and wild streets of the Bronx or to be confined to what was waiting for me in the wings.

John was buried at St. Raymond's Cemetery amongst our few family members. Being poor, my mother chose to bury him alongside of his father. My mother had married my dad when John's father died of cancer. I'm sure that my mom was not aware that she no longer would be able to be buried alongside her first husband. Laws had changed and the plot was not designed to hold three people. This would prove to be a sad mistake later on. It was after the funeral that I realized my mother would never accept the loss of her first-born child. Her alcoholic tendencies became more apparent and more frequent. She started drinking when people were waking to their morning coffee. About a year after John's death she was diagnosed with cirrhosis of the liver. I did not know then that it meant a death sentence. I just decided to put all my trust in God. In December of 1963, I spent the entire month cooking, cleaning and hanging out in the streets while my mother laid in a hospital bed at St. Francis Hospital across the street from our tenement on 142nd Street and Brook Avenue. No one knew that my brother and I were alone. A strong-willed, eleven-year-old and her twelve-year-old brother were on their own to do what they wanted, when they wanted. I used to tell those who asked that my mom had the flu and was staying in bed. My only relatives at the time were an aunt and cousins, and my brother's wife Rose and her two children. They were the only ones aware of the situation. What could anyone do to help? We had to just live alone and hope for the best. They did make sure that we had food, and continued to tell me not to let people know of our dilemma. Christmas was so lonely that year. My brother and I stayed in and watched television. I will never forget how pathetic our tree looked, which we decorated with the broken ornaments that had been smashed through the years. When my parents fought there were no limits to the destruction. That wasn't as bad as the fact that there was absolutely nothing under the tree, no gifts to give, no gifts to receive. Nothing! No one even stopped by that day. I suppose that is why through my children's lives I have always made Christmas the most important holiday of the year and my brothers' children. They receive at least twenty packages each, it is my reminder of the childhood that left such scars that would eventually surface time after time during my life.

On February 12, 1964, Mom passed away. When they took her to the hospital in an ambulance, they contacted social services to have us placed in someone's care. She left behind two children who would now remain alone permanently. I guess she could not control her want of alcohol and it overruled her sense of motherhood. Of course, I was bitter that she did not care enough for us to fight her disease. A disease that eats away at your soul and takes away the pain temporarily. Without drinking, an alcoholic cannot get through the day. It was much later on in my life after having children of my own that I would finally understand the loss she had suffered. It didn't take long for my aunt to place us in an orphanage. On June 6, 1964, I carried all that was left of my childhood in one suitcase up the two-mile road of the Mission of the Immaculate Virgin. Most people know it better as Mount Loretto, which is nestled in the outskirts of Staten Island. It took three hours by train, ferry and bus to reach my new home. That day will be etched in my mind and heart forever. I have always wondered, how you give away your blood relatives so soon after the devastating lost of a father, older brother and mother within four years? The harsh reality sent me searching for replacements for my loss. I had to have a family I kept telling myself until I reached Mount Loretto. Then I realized how many kids were just like me and had no one to tuck them in at night either. I searched for that family which was now gone. I wanted so desperately to belong to a family that was not dysfunctional and that would care for me and my brother as it should have been. It never happened during my teen years. I grew up in the shelter of nuns and priests who were trying to give attention to over one thousand homeless children. What could I expect from those odds? I would kneel on my knees at night and ask God, why? Why did this happen to us? The answers were all to come, not at my timing but when God thought it would be time to let me see that everything is not what it appears. I didn't know at that time that your path is set for you when you are born. I believed that God had set a path of life for me which would become a better way of living than I had been used to. Everything in life takes time, I was just a kid and for the life of me I could not understand why I had been sentenced to this confinement.

Chapter Three

"The Mount"

When I disembarked from the bus at Mount Loretto, my brother was ushered to the right, and I onto this long winding road on the left. I stood at the bus stop watching my brother walking away and wondered, how will I find him amid all the buildings? Will someone tell me where he is going, please? I asked. There was no response. Little did I know I would not see my brother for the next month. This was their policy in hopes of adjusting to the new environment and the sad separation of two siblings. No matter how many times they told me this was best for both of us, I counted down the days to again see him. At the end of the roadway was a beautiful view of the Raritan Bay. I walked toward the entrance to this large six-story building where I was greeted by a priest and two nuns. Later they were identified to me as Father Mangan, a wonderful man with a heart, Sister Jean Marie, whom I thought was the devil incarnate, and Sister Claire who was sweet and kind. The next few weeks caused me devastating harm as I was the new kid on the block and initiations are painful. I went from a bully from the South Bronx to the victim in the outskirts of Staten Island.

The first week at my new home found me robbed of all the decent clothing I possessed, the few dollars that my aunt left with me, and the Mickey Mouse wristwatch that my dad gave me the Christmas before he died. That watch was so important to me. Each night I would place it back in its red velvet box and remember that Christmas morning that Daddy came home after a long time away and handed it to me. I originally thought the gift was the box until Daddy showed me how to open it. It was the most beautiful gift I had ever received. Now on a cold winter morning, I awoke to find the case and the watch gone. I had this temper tantrum and was finally silenced by Sister Jean Marie, smacking me in the face. I had been this independent, street-wise kid from the South Bronx who thought I knew everything, thought I could do anything. The one thing I had little of was discipline. Well, I was about to be taught what happens when you don't listen. I must have had twenty beatings during that first month. Most of the beatings were as a result of my carrying my bible everywhere I went. My older brother John had bought it for me on the streets in New York. It seemed strange that, instead of this catholic facility encouraging me to increase my faith, I was being reprimanded for believing and reading God's word. I read it each day searching for an answer to why all of this had happened to my brother and me. I wanted to blame someone, but who? Sister Jean Marie would find me on the swings reading my book of books, when I was supposed to be in class. Eventually my bible was taken from me and not returned until I moved to the building called "The Villa."

I used to rise to the sound of a hand-rung bell at six in the morning. We would all march out in our sleep and kneel in the hallway and begin morning prayers. It lasted about ten minutes but to me it was forever since I spoke to God in my own way and time. Often I would lean up against the wall and fall back to sleep. That would not last too long because Sister Jean Marie would give me a whack to my head and awaken me for the second time. The day would then begin. Breakfast was on the first floor in a large cafeteria setting where we would have cold cereal, hot milk, and stale bread. I wondered what normal people were having for breakfast. Each group was assigned counselors of which I remember them all to have been nice college students. They would take us on walks to the town of Pleasant Plains, through the woods by the cemetery. If you had money, you could purchase treats. But who had money? I wasn't too good at hiding my personal properties. The days passed, and finally I was told I could see my brother. Visiting with siblings was every Thursday from three to four p.m., and then again on Sunday from ten to eleven-forty-five a.m. It was so unbearable to be separated from someone that I had counted on during my whole life. When I saw him, I ran to him and cried, "I'm leaving." I then told him, "I'm running away."

"Where are you going to go?" he responded. "They don't want us, and there is no other place to go." He told me it will get better, as he seemed to have been adjusting a lot better than I. I guess it helped that he was six foot three. He frightened people. I had no fight left in me by this point in time. When it was time for him to go, I watched him walk down that long winding road remembering how lonely I was without him. I believed that the sickening feeling I had was never going to go away. I went back to my dormitory and cried, still thinking that my best bet was to run away. One Sunday about two months after I arrived at this institution, I was informed that my aunt had come to spend the day and brought lunch. Oh, how I resented what she had done to my brother and me. She put us here, she never cared what happened because it wasn't her problem. When I arrived to the picnic area, she had set up the entire table with some cloth napkins, etc., and brought the typical Italian dinner, pasta and meatballs. Not even a kiss, she had no connection to me other than blood nor did she ever console me during all the times I needed someone. All these thoughts were running through my mind, when suddenly I took my hand and flung it toward the table, unable to stop my anger. Before I realized what I had done, I looked at all the food on the ground and just ran back to my little corner in the large dormitory realizing that Jerry was right, they did not want us in their lives. I did tell her before I ran that if I wasn't good enough to sit at her table and eat, I don't need her to ever come here again. You put me here, if I'm hungry, it's your fault, live with it. I cried myself to sleep that night hoping that when I awoke this whole scenario would have been a dream. It wasn't, it was oh so real.

The summer was nearing an end when I was summoned to the office. I was told they had received my school records and although the last year was not impressive, since I had been skipped in the third grade my overall average entitled me to attend an outside school. I was told I would be moved to the "Villa." This was like being in the Ritz Carlton verses a Rodeway Inn. There were only six girls in one dormitory versus the twenty-eight I had been subjected to since my arrival. The building was new, with matching curtains and bedspreads. I met Sister Augustine, an aging nun who was always with her dog, whose name I cannot recall. He was cute though. He was small and lovable, a lot like my Peaches today, a blonde Shit-zu with a lot of personality. The other nun was Sister Agnes Marie, known now as Sister Helen McNally, who teaches at St. Joseph By The Sea Catholic High School where two of my sons attended. I was a devil, and I gave her a rough time, but today when we meet, we just smile at each other. She straightened me out really quick, a normal punishment would be grounding me to the "Mount" for a month at a time, and I eventually learned but not without consequence. The "Villa" was for all of the "Mount" kids who were going to go to school off the premises. I attended Tottenville High School, made some lifetime friends and was able to see my brother every day since he attended school there also. Things were starting to get better, not great, just better. I had become friends with a girl named Carol. She was my best buddy. I could tell her anything. She brightened my life during those "Mount" days with her comical sense of humor and eventually she started to date my brother which brought us closer still.

I liked going to school off the grounds because I had a sense of freedom, the freedom I had grown up with, the freedom of knowing that I could survive on my own if I had to. When I think back to those days in the South Bronx, I never answered to anyone, sadly though because there was no one to answer to. My mom, by twelve each day, had drunk herself into oblivion and forgot that she had children that needed her. But I guess I didn't need her so much because I enjoyed the freedom of being on my own.

At Mount Loretto, the regimen was strict and schedules were followed. Up at six, mass at six-forty-five, breakfast at seven-fifteen and off to school by eight. Bed time during the week was nine-thirty p.m. and on weekends ten p.m. I know you must all be thinking I'm joking, but I assure you I'm not. We had but one television, so when you think it is rough when two people cannot agree on a show to watch, picture thirty girls agreeing on something. It sounds tough but it finally became a ritual and it didn't bother me anymore. I figured why fight it, as I was going to be there until my high school graduation four years away. So I just sat back and waited for better days to come.

Chapter Four

My Life As It Was

My new school reminded me of the school I attended in the Bronx. The building had three floors, clean, but it still was not home. I still longed for my mother and considered running away many times, as in the past. My aunt did not want me, and my sister-in-law Rose was unable to help. My brother John had left her with two babies to raise alone. If she could, she would have taken Jerry and me because her heart is made with gold. She was also still grieving the devastating loss of her husband. One day, while in the chapel, I realized God was trying to make me whole again. I envisioned that he stood before me and asked that I find happiness at my new home. A feeling of warmth surrounded me at that time, a feeling that I have come to know during the past forty years whenever I have felt there was no hope.

As the years passed at Mount Loretto, I made lifetime friends, found my first boyfriend and married the second. My husband, Patrick, was also raised in Mount Loretto since the age of eight. He used to milk the cows he told me. He and his older brother Robert, who died two years ago from a heart attack, set fire to their home in Brooklyn while their mom was out drinking. The court system intervened and placed both of them in Mount

Loretto. He too was lonely and frightened but once again he also had his brother to remind him of the life that once was. Some memories die hard. Even when most of them are not pleasant memories, they still stay etched in your heart and mind.

In 1967, after three long years at Mount Loretto, I once again felt emptiness as the war in Vietnam was to take my brother to another part of the world. I was heartbroken and asked Father Mangan to please do whatever he could to keep my brother from the conflict. As soon as I asked, the task was done. My brother was the last surviving son to carry on the family name. The court granted that he not be drafted into the service. I was so happy until I told him. He told me, "Sis, I love you. You will be fine, but a man has to serve his country during a time like this." He had enlisted the day before. Two weeks later, he left for Fort Benning, Georgia, and three months after that he arrived in Chu Lai, Vietnam. I prayed harder every day and asked that God not take away the one person left in my life that I counted on. Besides, he was the only person left of my real world.

I was about to begin my senior year at school and was looking forward to graduating. I could not wait for my long-awaited dream of starting a new life outside the confines of an institution. I was so regimented in my routine that I could not imagine getting up when I wanted, going to bed at two in the morning and choosing what would be best in my life. I would be able to eat what I wanted to eat and make decisions based on my dreams and not those that others had for me. Little did I know that the road that I would pave during the next few years would bring me to where I had always wanted to be. Tucked away in my heart I knew God was going to see me through. It is written in the bible that God would protect the widows and orphans of the world. I was so happy for Jerry, Rosie and myself. I believed that our salvation was a guarantee. I rarely admitted that I was an orphan, since I felt belittled. Had I told people they would ask why the rest of my family didn't want me, and why go into the whole story. It would not have served any purpose for them or for me. My friends at school, those that became my real friends, knew my situation but never looked down upon me. One friend, Susan, determined to have me come for her pajama party, had her parents get letters from their Lutheran Church to permit me to spend the night. Catholics always frowned upon other religions back in the sixties, especially the administration at Mount Loretto which could not comprehend a Catholic girl spending the weekend in the presence of a Lutheran family. So Susan's mom promised to take me to a Catholic Church on Sunday morning. It was the beginning of a lifetime friendship and sisterhood. Ironically, my other friend was also Susan from Tottenville. We still see each other often although she lives in Wyoming with her husband and three grown children. I get to see her at least once a year because her husband's family still lives in Staten Island. She just invited us to her daughter's wedding in Denver in October and I'm determined to get on that plane.

Still, the one friend that has been with me through it all is Carol. Carol and I were inseparable at Mount Loretto. I even thought she would someday marry my brother and we would truly be family. That didn't happen but our friendship never faltered and no matter how different our roads turned, they always lead back to each other. Today she lives in upstate New York but we talk at least once or twice a month. She will always be my Carol Ann. She will always be Auntie Carol to my children. Carol left Mount Loretto at the same time as my brother, so I had to face a double loss. Other friends came and went, and during reunions at the Mount, I can see many of them that I rarely see any other time during the year.

It was graduation day before I knew it. My brother was still in Vietnam but he had become a sergeant and was about to be transferred to Germany. Life was starting to look up, maybe there was the possibility of being happy, maybe God knew all along the road he would have me follow and follow I did, for happiness was about to become reality. My aunt and cousins came for the graduation but I missed having my brother there with me. He called to congratulate me and promised he would remain safe until his transfer. Here I was all dressed in white, feeling like the rest of my graduating class. That day I wasn't an orphan, I was one of them, I had earned the respect of the friends I had come to know and trust. My lifestyle did not come into view on that day as it often did when I would hear others talking about the "Mount" kids. The time had once again come for me to pack my suitcase, the same suitcase that brought me here four years ago. I was seventeen, ambitious and free from all the rules and guidance that had molded me into the stronger person that I had become. I was going to succeed, I was going to have it all, I was on my way back down that long winding road which led me to safety so many years before. In my pocket I had fifty dollars to begin my new life, but it felt like a million. I had a job waiting for me in New York where I would become a bank teller at Bankers Trust on Wall Street. I was looking forward to becoming my own person permanently and hoping that life would just begin to be a little happier.

Chapter Five

The Road To A New Life

Unfortunately, my first choice of housing in the real world did not lead to happiness. I had resided with a family where I rented a room shared with another. How I wanted my own room, something that would be just for me. I paid twenty-five dollars a week in rent, and I helped the family clean, cook and care for their children. That was in addition to my job at the bank in the city. Was this the price one paid for sharing in a family? Was I being used? Or was this the way it was supposed to be? I was not happy because this family came with more rules, more responsibilities and little gratification. It seemed I had gone from one institution to another. They also owned a grocery store which they expected me to help out in after working in the city all day and then again on the weekends. I had no life of my own. So once again I packed that suitcase and moved into an apartment with a friend from Mount Loretto. We had been close the last year at Mount Loretto and decided we could manage an apartment together. It was fun, we had pajama parties every night and traveled together to work in New York each day. It lasted for about nine months when she had decided that her boyfriend needed to spend more time with her and constantly stayed at the apartment. Pat would come over but never stayed the night since he was living with a couple who was teaching him responsibility and trying to make him part of their family. He shared a home with a couple who down the road would become Grandma and Grandpa to our children. John And Marjorie had lost their only son in Vietnam. Their house was quiet and were contacted by a friend asking if they would be interested in having a young man from Mount Loretta stay with them. That was the beginning of a relationship that would keep them in our lives and in the lives of our children forever. Our grandpa died last year but not without giving us the family we desperately searched for all those years ago. I decided I had to find somewhere else once again to live and as usual God was with me that day. While boarding the Staten Island ferry, I ran into Susan. It was Susan, whose family took me home for weekends of family times during my senior year at high school. Susan told me her sister got married and she wanted to know if I wanted to live with her and her family. I went that night to speak with her parents and the next week I finally became part of a family that would see me through the next thirty years. I guess the Lutherans were as kind as the Catholics after all. The following day was my birthday and they gave me presents. Real presents. I can still remember a leather bag patched in different colors and Susan bought me a little statue for my dresser.

Pat and I were still growing closer. We went out on weekends dancing and what today is called clubbing. We learned to dance so well together. Pat got his first car and we began going to visit the little bit of family that he had. His older brother lived out in Long Island, somewhere off of the Long Island Expressway. They were a little surprised that he showed an interest in rekindling his relationship with his older estranged brother. They too showed little interest in seeing us very often. His brother Robert, whom we called "Bob," decided to join the Navy. With my brother in Germany and his brother out on an aircraft carrier, we grew all the closer. Susan and I had great times together. Her parents treated me so kind. I never had to do anything except keep my room neat which was no problem for me since I had become a perfectionist during my "Mount" days.

Pat was always welcomed to come over and during the year I spent with Susan and her family I had become a true member of it. Christmas for the first time in my life had some meaning. I started to understand why families came together at the holidays. We would laugh, have some wine, play games in the street and with each passing day I began to watch my dream of having a family unfold before me. They even bought me a pile of Christmas gifts. Susan's parents became Mom and Dad Boye. They were so kind and caring to bring this troubled teenager to their home and work so hard to make me happy and happy I became. I came into myself. I realized I had a great sense of humor, a great will to care for people and that I cherished the deeper love I felt for Pat. I believed this was the real thing, and I was ready to make a commitment. I wondered if I would be good for him, if would he be good for me, and if could we build on the existing relationship and make it last. Those years of dreaming were starting to become a reality. Pat was the kindest guy, cute, with a great smile, nice voice and the whole world loved him. He was definitely a better person than I. The decision was about to be made whether we were ready yet to let go of the institution we had left and enter into the institution of marriage. He proposed in the fall of 1969 with the blessings of my brother. We planned to marry in September of 1970. This would give us enough time to save money and have a memorable wedding. I would search for a white gown, decide on my wedding party and plan a big reception for our family and friends. We were so much in love, we had the same dreams, the same past, and our hearts knew we could have a great future as long as we continued to dream it together. For once in my life, I had someone who needed me. That is how we both felt and chose to dance to that song on our wedding day.

Our plans were shared with our Grandma and Grandpa and my Mom and Dad Boye. We rented a hall, hired a photographer and received permission to marry at the Church of St. Joachim & Anne on the grounds of Mount Loretto. We would continue on from where it had all began. I called my brother in Germany and told him he had to come home to walk me down the aisle. He promised he would not miss it for the world. I promised to write with all the plans so that he could feel as much a part of the preparations even though he was thousands of miles away. I was happy, Pat was happy and together the plans began to fall into place.

Chapter Six

The Wedding Day

It was a day to remember. My best friends, my brother, my niece Rosemarie, nephew John, and of course the bride and groom ready to celebrate this day of days. My bridesmaids looked so great in their gowns of assorted pastel shades of blue, pink, lavender and green. I ordered them parasols to match, we didn't know it then that they were going to need umbrellas on that rainy day. The men were so handsome in their tuxedos. My brother crying like a baby and my nephew holding on to me like I was going to my death. Excuse me everyone, this is supposed to me a happy day! We were married by both Father Mangan and our family friend Father Budwick. I was told years later that they had placed a bet that our marriage would last forever. The church reminded us of yesterdays, my confirmation and the funerals for our lost friends from the "Mount." Many died in Vietnam. Today would be for new memories, ones that would carry us through to the next generation. I knew I loved him and I knew he loved me. Father Budwick had served at the Mount for a few years and because he was so young and good looking the girls really enjoyed his stories and his determined desire to make a difference for all those there at Mount Loretto. He had left the

Mount the same year that my brother went to Vietnam. During a final farewell, the girls at the Mount put on a show to entertain him. Carol and I sang "To Sir With Love" to him. He was totally moved by the dedication and the rest is history. Pat and I were married during a mass at St. Joachim & Ann, and I knew that if I started my marriage with God at my side, he would bless our years together. When we were pronounced man and wife, we practically danced back down the aisle. We greeted all one-hundred-and-fifty guests who came to share in our happy day and couldn't wait for the party to follow.

We then headed to our reception at the Harmony House which was adjacent to where my husband worked at the Staten Island Advance. Today it is called the Island Chateau. The rain refused to let up, it was misty, a damp day in September but it sure held up to the saying that if it rains on your wedding day, you will be able to endure all. We danced, we laughed, we visited with those we had not seen in awhile. It was to be the beginning of a life of security and adventure. When the clock finally struck twelve the party was over and the marriage was about to begin. Yes, "For Once in My Life," a song written and performed by Stevie Wonder. I finally had someone who needed me. To show you how it all worked out, this is a poem I wrote for him this past Valentine's Day. I wrote him many poems during our time together, but this was different because this time I knew that I would never question again the love I had for him in my heart.

February 14, 2002

Heart To Heart (For My Husband)

Today we should be able to look to the sky
Strangers, lovers or maybe just you and I
Searching each day to renew strong desires
Thinking of days when we lit our own fires

It is a day for candies, flowers and laces
Those youthful days, those smiles on faces
The day we met and two hearts became bound
For love in each other we both had found

If ever we part, if one of us should leave
That would be the day unbearable for me
We traveled through the worst along our road
Together we survived and achieved our goal

After thirty-two years we have found new strength
More than we had before we first met
Behind us we look at a happy and long life
So lucky for me that you made me your wife

So stay by my side, as you have done in the past
Together we will make this love of ours last
Remember how I said that when one door closes
The next door to open will be filled with roses

Happy Valentine's Day to my one true love
Sent to me from the heavens above
I loved you then, now and through eternity
I'll be there for you as you have for me

Our honeymoon was inexpensive since our budget was tight after exhausting all we had to pay for our reception. We received a great surprise when my Mom and Dad Boye returned to me all I had paid in rent for the past year. Back then a wedding gift of a thousand dollars was equivalent to ten thousand today. We choose a place in the Poconos' called Honeymoon Hideaway. It really turned out to be a hideaway, as it should have taken us two hours to get there and after six hours we decided to contact them. They were kind, came to rescue us from our dilemma. We are probably the only honeymooners who had the priest that married them come and spend a day with us on our honeymoon. We all went out to dinner and marked it as one of the most unusual visits anyone probably had. We had a great time. Father Budwick was an associate at a parish in nearby Ellenville, New York. The activities included horseback riding, archery, games, contests and all with twenty other couples who were married on the same day. Upon leaving our little hideaway we vowed to someday return, maybe at a time when we would have forgotten those precious first days together. We never did return and frankly I don't believe it even exists anymore.

After our week of vacation from the world, we returned to our new apartment on Edgegrove Avenue in Huguenot. We had a basement apartment which was just completed prior to our moving in. This was our home. It belonged to us. It was beautiful, our new furniture, new life, happy and content. All we needed now was a puppy and a puppy we got. We named her Kischa after an African ship. At the time I had been working for a shipping firm and had everyone enter a name to be drawn on the day we would make her part of our new life. It was as though I was having a baby. Kischa was half Collie and half German Shepherd, very smart and oh so lovable. We took her everywhere with us. Her unconditional love for us bonded us together as if it was all meant to be. So this was the real world, we worked, shopped and entertained our friends since we were the first to marry and have our own place.

On our first anniversary we chose to spend a week down the shore in Wildwood with another couple. We rented a house, a few houses from the beach. How romantic it was, to wake to the sound of the waves, soak in the sun all day, have dinner and walk the shore line at night. Pat and I loved the ocean and vowed that someday we would own a place. Dreams do come true if you really believe in them. We had just purchased a 1965 Chevrolet Impala Convertible, my husband's dream car. We loved that car until it was stolen in 1972 and we found it totaled deep in the woods of Great Kills Park. It was hard to replace it but we surpassed our loss and purchased a bomb just to continue our leisurely rides around town.

We spent our second anniversary on a well-deserved trip to Las Vegas, Hawaii and San Francisco. We felt like we were on the top of the world. It was the greatest vacation, and Hawaii was the most beautiful place Pat and I had ever seen. We took an airplane excursion to six islands in twenty-four hours. We were exhausted but it was the only way we could have seen so much in so little time, on a limited budget. When our third anniversary came around, we decided to visit our friends, Sue and Cliff, who were living in Arizona at the time and agreed to vacation in the Grand Canyon. The only downfall of our trip was that the night prior to our trip, I was informed I was pregnant with our first child. We decided not to tell anyone until we returned the following week. We were thrilled, we had saved my paycheck all along and were in a position to support a child. We were twenty-three and felt we were mature enough to bring a special addition to our family.

We spent nights and days trying to decide what we would name our child. We finally agreed that if it was a boy we would name him Brian and if it was a girl we would call her Johnna after my brother who died. Well on May 24, 1974, Brian Patrick was born on his due date. I'm always on time with everything. He would be the first of our three sons, our first child, the first time that something truly belonged to us, a gift from God. We adored him and vowed to give him a life filled with love and nurturing. We knew that we would work hard to give this child the many important things that we had both been denied.

I think it was the day that we realized the wedding was over, the trips were a thing of the past, and our anniversaries would now be celebrated with a special dinner. It was no problem giving it all up, for in return we had a son, a creation made from the love that we shared. Our dreams now were for him and his future.

We moved into our first home six months after Brian was born. In 1979, we raised the roof of the two-bedroom house and built up another floor. Now we were totally prepared for the additional children we planned to have. It was after Brian was born that my aunt and cousins decided they wanted to be a part of Brian's life, which would mean they would once again be part of mine. It was as if they finally realized that I was a person that I had feelings and needed love in my life too. By this time, I had slowly matured into a young, responsible lady who knew what I wanted and knew I had to make the life of my first born, a life where he would never be ashamed to tell people who he was, as I did during my teen years at the "Mount." I saw that my aunt and cousins wanted to give back to Brian all that they denied my brother and me. Sometimes it is so hard to forget and forgive those who hurt you, but life goes on and forgiveness must always play a significant role, because without it, no one moves on. I no longer feel any animosities toward my aunt, actually. I visit her often at the nursing home in Brooklyn. She chose to put me in a home instead of welcoming me into hers. I told myself to get past it and start looking at my tomorrow instead of remembering the yesterdays. With the birth of Brian, I was determined to put the past in the past. I wanted everyone to enjoy this bundle of joy that God gave to Pat and me. We visited my aunt and cousins often in Brooklyn and Brian enjoyed the attention that was given to him as a baby. They loved seeing him and I often looked at them and thought, maybe they really do care, maybe things worked out for the best. I thought of how difficult I had been and maybe my aunt knew she was unable to deal with two troubled teens. I knew at this time I could forget and just maybe the pain and hurt they caused me would be buried once and for all.

The bible tells us "if you hold something bound, it is held bound." My life was okay, and I really did want Brian to grow up knowing his few biological family members. Later I found out that blood is not thicker than water for my relationship with Grandma today could be no more solid if she had been Pat's biological mother.

Grandma and Grandpa taught us so much about life. The things someone should have told us when we were younger. Their version was more interesting and we learned so much about the love of family through their wisdom. There were many times during holiday periods where we needed to choose who to spend them with. The real or the perceived. We always tried to be fair and share the time with all.

Chapter Seven

The Family We Became

As planned, Daniel John, our second son arrived on January 22, 1980, a total of twenty-seven days late. He was small, a mere five pounds and two ounces, but as beautiful as they come. It had been six years since I gave birth to Brian, and it was like starting all over again. I was working at the time as a vice-president of a service bureau in Staten Island. It was so difficult leaving this tiny baby each day and my heart would break each morning when I kissed him goodbye. His nanny said as soon as he realized I had left, he would stop crying and become the little devil he truly was and continues to be. She had to follow him all over as he got older because he would get into everything. I continued to work up until the birth of our third son, Keith Gerard, on November 16, 1981. It was almost like I had twins, so close together, it was difficult financially but for them it was a blessing. They adored their older brother and together they formed a bond that I truly believe no one will ever break. They fought as most siblings do, but I think in sharing their childhood they grew closer because of it. To this day, the only time we see them truly laugh and enjoy life is when they are together.

As they grew older, they grew closer. Each went to the other's baseball games, basketball games, they watched TV together and we all vacationed each year in Ocean City, Maryland. Their memories of growing up together are still talked about today. Grandma and Grandpa are the greatest part of their memories. Grandpa, who died almost two years ago, just adored them all. He took them fishing, taught them how to canoe, or I should say tried to teach them, and they were a part of their everyday lives as Grandma continues to be today. I say Grandma and Grandpa because that's who they were to our children. Once again, the story of my husband and my life found us always in search of a real family when we left the "Mount." Pat lived with Grandma and Grandpa until we married and by then our relationship was on an incline.

During the funeral mass for Grandpa, as the priest spoke of this man's extreme qualities as a good Christian and his undying morality, the sobbing from a few rows back became more obvious. When the sobs continued, I was gently tapped on the shoulder from the pew behind me at Our Lady Queen of Peace Church in New Dorp by a family member, informing me that the sobbing was that of my children. It was so hard for these young people to say goodbye to this man who helped to raise them into the responsible young adults they have become today. It took a long while for those sad goodbyes, remembering the songs of spiritual renewal and the shock of Grandpa's heart attack to pass. The sadness in our lives was obvious but we knew we needed to be strong in order to care for Grandma. She was feeling lonely and very frightened. We knew things would be different now since Grandpa did most of the running of their home. Grandma suffers with a sight problem that causes a lack of balance. We knew she would require more of our love and dedication than before. She always feels as though she is a burden to us, but to us she was heaven-sent. She always says the right things at the perfect time and is always there when we need someone to rely on for advice. Keith is very close to her and that was true of Grandpa also. Brian is married to a wonderful woman named Vikki. Our son Daniel now resides in the state of Maryland. Keith stays close to home to keep my husband, grandma and I in line. One day while we were up in the mountains, Grandma decided that the men should all go on a canoe trip. To make a long story short, it is the story of stories in our family. Grandpa went with Keith, and my husband went with Daniel. Five minutes into the trip, Keith catapulted Grandpa right out of the canoe by standing up and reaching for his sneaker which dropped in the water. He did it two more times during their four-hour adventure and I have never seen Grandpa so mad. Later on that evening at dinner, when Grandpa told his version of the story, we laughed for hours. It was that day that Keith and Grandpa became best friends, and the story of canoes became the family favorite. Time after time, it was told and each time the story became funnier and funnier. Even today, with Grandpa gone almost two years, the story has a way of coming up every now and then. Those are the kinds of memories that make a family a family.

Chapter Eight

The Grandma And Grandpa Story

From a distance, you could see the two of them walking through the town of New Dorp, Staten Island on their daily walk. I should rephrase it as their daily hike. I had always admired them especially because they stuck together after the sad death of their only son, "Jan," who died in Vietnam in 1968. As the story was told, Jan was missing for a few weeks prior to his return to them for burial. Our Grandpa always said, "he did what he had to do." Jan chose to enter the military and serve his country through the Vietnam Conflict. He was Grandpa and Grandma's life and their only child. I can remember the first time I met them, when I was seventeen years old and had no idea of the joy of a child, no less the loss of one, but it reminded me of the anguish my mother must have suffered when my brother passed away. I almost felt that their pain was more than I could bear. How dare I? It was their loss and not mine. I should be able to face them and share in their pain. It was difficult as Grandpa spoke little about the circumstances and Grandma's eyes shed so many tears when she would tell us stories about him. I never would have imagined the importance of these two people in my children's lives. We were giving them grandchildren they would never have had, and we now had grandparents for our children. We gave to them grandchildren that I think in some small way eased their pain during the following years. God does provide all we need.

As the years passed and the children kept them hopping, we became true family. I pray that the boys helped them to think of the good times and gave them a little happiness that was denied them due to Jan's death. The relationship was more than either of us could have asked for. It wasn't until Keith and Daniel were sixteen years old that they finally realized who Grandma and Grandpa truly were. We never disrespected them nor did the children. We went to New Orleans for Palm Sunday in 1998. It was just about the best trip we had ever taken, and Grandma and Grandpa enjoyed the Bayou. We took a river boat ride down the Mississippi and toured the infamous Bourbon Street. Memories that no one can take away, happy memories.

Every Columbus Day weekend we would spend in the mountains of Andes, New York. It was a three-and-a-half-hour drive to the mountain cottage. It was small, but had a lot of love in it. We would fly kites, fish, sit and talk and await Grandma's famous hot dogs and chili for dinner. We slept down in the town at the Andes Hotel since the cottage was small and not totally updated with all plumbing and electrical amenities. It was a house filled of love, of memories, fifteen years of memories, those we shared with just Grandma and Grandpa. It was that holiday weekend every year that we grew to love each another and without the words ever being uttered, we knew that we would always be family, whether biological or not, we shared a special bond that no one could ever take away. I once told Grandma that God put us together so that our children would have the relationship that most families have. It is so ironic that when I think back to my childhood today, I realize that one child's mistake can pull a whole family apart as it had back in the South Bronx, a lifetime ago. How fortunate for us that Grandma and Grandpa entered our lives.

All of our friends admired them also. When we would introduce them to anyone, we finally just said "this is Grandma and Grandpa. Then the whole family started calling them Grandma and Grandpa. Now that we only have Grandma left, we cling to each day, enjoying her wisdom and virtues in fear that someday she will leave us also. She knows how much we love her and want her in our everyday lives, not out of obligation, but just out of love. She is one fine lady who just celebrated her 85th birthday. We surprised her with a party at Jade Island Restaurant and invited many of her childhood friends and family. She had a great time and she knows that we will be there for her always. She is full of grace and she is a special Grandma because she gave her love out of want and not out of need.

Chapter Nine

World Trade Center Tragedy

It was a beautiful morning traveling to work from Staten Island on the Verrazano Bridge. The sun was just coming up and the beauty of the sky was breathtaking. The blue skies were lined with shades of orange and white. I sat up in the bus and gazed out over the open waters at the beauty that lied before me. I enjoyed this twenty-minute trip each morning. Since the traffic was behind us, it was a quick way of getting to work by six a.m. By the time the bus arrived at Vesey Street, the sun was brightly shining. I bid farewell to my girlfriend, Marie, who worked on the 25th floor of Tower One. We had been commuting together for the past three years. We traveled back and forth together on the bus because our hours were the same. Early to rise was our motto. What I wouldn't give to have those days back again. I walked to my building a few steps from the bus stop and unlocked the main door. I looked back for a second to look again at the beautiful blue sky and the peace that reigned upon me in the early morning hours. It was a peaceful time when the city was just awakening and the silent noise of buses and cars were arriving for another hectic day in the metropolis of our country. I often think about that morning. What made me turn around and look up at those skies prior to entering the office building? Had one of my premonitions seemed too real on that sad Tuesday morning? I knew in my heart that it would be the last time I would feel a sense of peace here in downtown Manhattan. I could never have imagined how different my life was going to be as I turned and walked inside. I pressed the button to the eleventh floor and unlocked the doors to our office. I immediately had work left to do from the day before and began to type with my normal enthusiastic nature. It was about eight a.m. when my boss called and asked that I draft a document which he needed faxed to the Westchester office. I began to draft the pleading and was just about finished when above me was the roar of a plane as if its engines went dead and it was falling. I ran to the window of my office and saw the plane crashing into Tower One of the Trade Center. The vibration was felt so dramatically that the floor shook beneath me. I ran toward the front of the office and looked out the window at a ball of fire racing through the upper floors of the tower. I yelled to those in the office to get their bags and get out of the building. After locking the office, I ran down the eleven flights of stairs out onto the street in the front of the building.

The police were all over and the fire trucks were arriving in mass amounts. People were huddled in crowds trying to get up Vesey Street away from the towers. It was total bedlam. I watched the black smoke pouring from the building, thinking about those poor people who never had a chance to get out of the burning building. Then as I gazed up, I realized that the debris was becoming larger as it fell on the sidewalk beside me. We all stepped back a little further and continued to stare at this startling accident. After a few minutes, the flames became greater and I realized sadly that the debris falling onto the sidewalk in front of me was people and body parts. As I realized the extent of what I was watching, many more people were jumping to their death from the roof and windows of Tower One. I saw a group of five women, holding hands as they jumped together from an upper floor. As they came toward the ground, the bodies scattered in different directions. The policeman standing in front of our building told me that a small plane was caught in wind shear and crashed. The gapping hole led me to think it had to be something a little larger than a prop plane.

One employee was totally out of control, crying and screaming that she needed to be with her newborn baby, while another employee rushed off to save herself. She recently had a baby and was scared to death that she would not be able to get to the child. At that time I had no idea of the horror which was about to unfold during the next few hours. I was under control and felt secured knowing the police were by my side and if there was anything to worry about, they would make us aware of it. Little did I know the horror that was about to become reality as thousands of New Yorkers were about to make a desperate attempt to escape the downtown area.

The story begins…

Chapter Ten

Escaping The Terror

After watching so many people jumping to their deaths from the upper floors of Tower One, I decided I had seen enough and was about to go back up to my office when people started to scream. I turned in time to see the second plane full force crash into Tower Two. This plane sheared the entire corner of the building in a flash. I didn't need a policeman to tell me we were in trouble. Knowing immediately that this was no accident I began to run up Vesey Street with the crowds. The police were yelling to move quickly toward the river. People were being struck with flying metal and cement pieces coming from the towers. As I ran toward Broadway, keeping my head down, I could see shoes, pocketbooks and brief cases lying in the debris of dust and paper, as people knew that they only wanted to escape with their lives, nothing else was important during those first few minutes. I believe at least half of those running knew this was definitely a terrorist attack. What are the chances that two planes were caught in wind shear?

I remember the first few minutes during my attempted escape. A bicycle messenger was riding along the side of me when he was struck in the head by a piece of flying metal. The policeman running along the side of me yelled to keep going, that "you can't help him, he is dead." Then my blood really began to pump thinking I could be next. When I think back now, I can't imagine how I stayed in control of myself. That quick moment was the true beginning of the terror I was about to experience. A terror that would follow me for the next year of my life. As the police and firemen continued yelling, "run to the river," my heart was pounding with vibrations of what would be next. I wondered why they were telling us to run to the river. I know no one expected what was about to occur during the next forty five minutes.

As the mass exit of people continued running across Broadway, the debris thickened with each step. Trying to look ahead and not down, trying to avoid the sights that surrounded me, I struggled to keep running in the clog hoppers I had chose to wear that day. I stopped when I reached Broadway and noticed that the streets were covered in ash and office papers that once sat on employees desks were now scattered all over the ground and continued pouring from the skies. The odor was beginning to become more apparent as the tears and horror on the faces of those near me made me take a second hold of myself, if only to catch my breath. I looked back at the burning of those towers and quickly looked around me at the tremendous horror unfolding. People were crying, men were holding women as they continued to flee and yet the continued screaming of thousands made me realize the fear other countries must live with on a regular basis. How could this happen? Who could have done such a horrific act, knowing they would kill thousands of hardworking, innocent people? The first plane, striking at eight-fifty a.m., found many employees already at their desks. There were constant blasts of noises that continued as the roar of the flames became greater. I realized I needed to get further than one block from this disaster although the crowds were not moving, it made sense that at some point evacuating such a large area would be difficult on the narrow streets leading toward the City Hall area. The police and firemen were trying to get the crowds to move down to the river. I remember like it was yesterday, those words echoing in my mind, and I dreamt for days and months after, "run to the river." *Why run to the river? Was I going to have to jump into the river to survive?* As I continued to slowly move along, down Ann Street toward Nassau Street, I thought of my family. I needed to reach them. I needed to tell them that I was alive. I reached for my cell phone only to see that there was no service. The need to let them know kept echoing in my mind. The lines for the few phones were fifty deep. *Did I have time to make a call? What do I do? Where should I go? Should I go into a building and ask for help?* I found myself weak from fear and yearning to go home. Whatever street you turned on, the people were running, the fire trucks and ambulances were trying to get through the melee with little avail. What could they have done anyway? It was obvious this was going to be one fire that would take a miracle to put out. I still never anticipated the events about to take place until the roar under my feet continued to keep my heart pounding at a rapid speed. As I continued down Fulton Street, I befriended a black woman who looked at me and wrapped her arms around me, saying: "We are going to get out of here." I must have had the look of death that made this stranger come toward me.

It was almost ten past ten when the entire area began to shake. At first, I thought another plane crashed, and without looking behind me, I just kept running. People were screaming that Tower Two had come down. The area thickened in a dark-gray smoke as it billowed through the already blackened sky as far as one could see. As soon as Tower Two went down the entire skies turned to black. You could hear people but you could not see them. After a few minutes everything turned black. I wasn't sure where I was in the following few seconds. I wanted to go toward the Staten Island Ferry but was ushered in the opposite direction. In the distance, voices were echoing that the ferry to Staten Island was closed. I kept thinking, *is this it? Are we all going to die as we continued running? Were we all going to die as we ran toward the river?* I ran as fast as I could in the shoes I had on. I eventually ran out of the blackness to look down and see this gray ash that covered my clothes and shoes. Where am I? I continued to follow the noise in front of me, and realized I was now running on cobblestones. I knew then I had to be in the Seaport area since it is the only place I can remember that cobblestone still lined the sidewalks. I continued to run along the water without stopping to breathe. I turned and saw that only one tower remained standing. I began praying, *please God, keep walking with me, and bring me safely home, wherever that will be, is entirely up to you.* Anyone with the slightest common sense at that point knew that if Tower Two went down, the same fate was in store for Tower One.

As I was nearing the Brooklyn Bridge, the police were turning us away from the entrance because the smoke had filled the area and they were unable to see the people on the bridge. Now, they yelled to go to the Manhattan Bridge. *Where am I going? Where is the Manhattan bridge?* I wondered. I kept running, following the crowd, then the crowd started dispersing upwards, back toward the Trade Centers. I began to panic, thinking, *I'm going the wrong way,* but was informed by a policeman that the entrance to the Manhattan Bridge was back four blocks. I hesitated, then followed the group that was around me. My feet were aching, my heart breaking, thinking of all those that I knew who worked in the towers and probably many had not made it to safety. Maybe they just haven't caught up to us. After all, I was on the street when they were still exiting the towers. When I reached a more secured area of many police cars, I began to feel like I would be okay. Then there was another large noise, I wasn't sure what it was, but the screaming and running began again. As I saw the entrance to the bridge, I needed to stop a second and get control. I have such a fear of heights. *How will I get over this bridge?* I thought to myself, and, *what waits for me on the other side?* I tried to use the cell phone again, trying to dial the 718 area code, but there was no response. I thought maybe if I tried a different area code I would have some success in reaching those that I knew were probably panicking without hearing from me. I tried the 908 area code in New Jersey, but there was no connection. It then dawned on me to try and reach our office in the Westchester County area. It worked. I heard the voice of my boss, asking, "Are you okay?" I said, "Yes, I'm about to walk across the Manhattan Bridge. Please call my family and tell them I'm trying to get home." He told me he would send a car to get me. I chuckled and realized he had no idea that the . city was in complete chaos, no cars would be getting in or out unless they had sirens attached to them. I knew that the only way I was going to get out was to walk across that bridge. As I started across, I could once again hear rumbling noises, and I wondered to myself what was happening back at what now is referred to as "Ground Zero."

I started to cross the bridge and was about halfway across when there was another noise, a massive noise, a noise that I knew I had heard once already today. As I reached the top of the bridge, I turned and in total disbelief watched in horror as Tower One disappeared into the ground. "Oh my God," I exclaimed; the towers have both come down. I leaned on the railing of the bridge, not knowing whether to cry, continue running, or just stay there and let whatever would happen to just happen. I did not know if I had any strength left to go on, when a voice said to me to keep going. I'm not sure who it was because at this point I started to enter a trance state and was hoping this was all just a nightmare and not really happening. I followed, very slowly behind the crowd, unable to move quickly due to the blisters digging into the back and bottom of my feet. I had to continue, I told myself, keep going when all of a sudden I felt as though I had new strength, as if there was another set of feet carrying me across that bridge. I never looked back after that, because I knew if I looked back that I would fail to go forward.

As I reached the other side of the bridge, I had no idea where I was except that I was in Brooklyn. The police lined the streets as the flocks of people walked onto what I know now was Flatbush Avenue. It was at that moment that I realized this tragedy was already uniting the people of New York. Store owners were handing out bottles of water to us as we continued our trek into safety. After perusing all the bus signs, I saw that the bus I needed was the M37, which would take me close to the Verrazano Bridge near Bay Ridge, Brooklyn. I knew if I could get to Bay Ridge, I could possibly cross over the Verrazano Bridge which would take me home to Staten Island.

The lines for the buses were hundreds long. Although, most stops serviced three or four different buses, I felt my chances of boarding one became slimmer as each bus passed, already loaded to capacity. It seemed like hours had passed, and I was still standing in line waiting for a bus to arrive and open its doors to this weary person in dire need of reaching home. Where was the origin point of these buses, I thought? I began to walk further up Livingston Street in search of a shorter line or the starting point. It was worse the farther up I traveled. I stood amidst the crowds just gazing at the people in disbelief. Thousands of people covered in ash, thousands in worst shape than I, who were still fleeing the downtown area in search of reaching a safe haven. We had no radios, no news of the survivors, I did not even know that the planes were ours until later on that night. *Oh please, God, help me get home,* I kept whispering to myself through my tears. As I looked up the street, I saw a woman with no clothes on, screaming, she was being escorted by what appeared to be her co-workers. A police emergency vehicle pulled over and swept the woman into the back of the vehicle. I thought to myself, *will she ever be okay?* I never figured I would eventually be asking myself the same question.

The hours were passing and a man was standing at the bus stop yelling that he was responsible for what happened. He blamed the government for stealing millions of dollars from him. He was a ragged-looking black man, who was ranting on in anger about the arrogant white women of New York. As he continued to yell about the white women, a group of black people began to shelter me from his sight. I loved them for it, as the last thing I needed at this time was to fear an individual who obviously was not in his right state of mind. An hour had passed and not one bus stopped to board anyone. I began to feel threatened because I had not made any progress of reaching my home in more than two hours. As I glanced across the street, I saw a bus with the number M37 heading in the opposite direction. Since traffic was at a near standstill, I had the opportunity to cross in between the vehicles and make it to the bus stop on the other side. I did not realize that people surmised what I had in mind and chose to follow me through the lanes of traffic leading to the bus which was standing just waiting for me to get on. The driver took one look at me and opened the door, and it was as if someone had given me a second chance. I boarded the bus along with fifty to sixty people who packed the bus immediately. As the bus crawled along Livingston Street, I had no idea where it was going, but I knew I was not getting off. This bus has to turn around and head back the opposite way, and the people and I agreed we would refuse to disembark at the end of the line. What else could go wrong! I was about to find out when the engine to the bus started hesitating about half way up Livingston Street. I figured this was the end of the line. I knew I felt like I was at the end of my line. I vividly remembered seeing thousands along the streets standing in disbelief, as I had waited to find refuge on this bus. Only I could have boarded a bus that would break down. By this time, another forty minutes had passed and now I had to get off this bus anyway. I did not know where I was but decided to follow the crowds. I remember looking up and seeing a sign that said Third Avenue, this was the road I walked on for what seemed like forever. The numbers were going up so I figured it was best to continue on. I was so determined to reach 86th Street near the Verrazano Bridge that I forgot about my feet and the pain radiating from them. I had a chance of getting over the bridge if it was open. There were emergency vehicles with deafening sirens, heading toward the bridges to try to rescue anyone they could. Buses were passing me by, packed front and back, and I envied those who were on those buses, as they were going to get further and faster than I would on foot. It was obvious that the drivers of these buses were feeling bad because they were unable to pick up any more riders. There were thousands of others who continued to walk along Third Avenue, hoping to see an empty bus come up behind us and take us to our destinations. My only other option was to stand still and wait. *Wait for what?* I thought. So I just continued following behind.

The trains were not running, cars could barely get through all the barricades so it was up to the bus drivers of the city to help evacuate those who had only made it across a bridge to safety. The buses were now edging along at a snail's pace. I waited anxiously for the numbers on the streets to reach higher, I remember 33rd, which were my children's lucky basketball number. I thought, *Could I possibly make it through the eighties?* Then I knew I could walk across the avenues until I reached the bridge leading to my home in Staten Island. As I tried my cell phone again, the busy signal continued to pound in my ear. I had hoped that my boss was able to reach my family, as it was now approaching three o'clock, and I had been escaping for six hours and was nowhere near to my home. Traffic all along 3rd Avenue was at a standstill. Finally, a bus opened its back door and fortunately I was right there and the first to hop on. As I hobbled onto the bus, I felt the tears filling my eyes. I had given every ounce of strength that I had in order to get this far. I just stood on the bus and looked out at nothing and for a while thought about nothing. The bus continued to open the back doors to those along the way. *Had I truly walked forty-seven blocks from the Manhattan Bridge, even though I hate to walk?* As each person huddled onto the already crowded bus, we made more and room for them, knowing we all shared the same fate that day and we needed to help each other. I glanced out the window at the storekeepers looking around wondering what was going on. *Was I dreaming? Why did they seem to be unaware of the day's events? Was I dreaming? Was it over? Or, did I just slip into a state of confusion?* When the bus reached 80th Street after what seemed like forever, I decided I would get off and try to walk the next few blocks. It was a good choice since the bus hadn't moved, as I glanced back and wondered what was holding up the flow of vehicles. As I approached 86th Street, the answer to my question was revealed. The Verrazano Bridge was closed to traffic. I uttered to myself, "God, please don't let this be, this is the only way home for me." I seemed to drift into another world as I continued to search for a bus leading to Staten Island.

At 86th Street and 5th Avenue, a kind driver who was just sitting on a bus with his engine in the off position opened his rear door and allowed me to get on along with a dozen others. As I edged my way through the already crowded bus, people began to stare at me. Questions began to be asked. "What happened to you? Why do you look as you do? Can you hear me?" I heard in a distance. With that occurring around me, a woman sitting in the rear of the bus stood up and offered me her seat. I knew I needed to sit down, so I rushed to occupy the empty space. I remember others telling the passengers on the bus of the events in New York, some were not aware that the towers had collapsed, that thousands were killed, that we had already spent six hours trying to reach the only safe place we knew— home! As I sat quietly in my two-by-four space, I began to shiver, I started to cry, I started to realize what I had been through and cried for those whose fate I did not know. Others began to console me, but I didn't hear their words yet I felt their compassion as they stared at my gray-covered dress and ash-covered body. I remember that I kept focusing on my shoes, knowing that I did not own dusty, gray shoes.

While sinking deeper into fear, I remember hearing the roar of the bus engine start up. *Did they finally open the bridge? Will they blow up the bridge as we cross over?* The fear was mounting as the bus began to move from its spot. The traffic on the Gowanus Expressway was as far back as one could see. There were so many vehicles trying to escape to a safe place by using the Verrazano Bridge. Many weary travelers were desperately trying to reach home, and whether they lived in Staten Island or New Jersey, they needed that bridge to open. I began to pray again, *Please Lord, let me cross in safety. Let me reach Staten Island so I can once again see my family.* Nothing was more important for me at that time, and nothing else mattered. I continued to hear people asking me questions, but my silence continued, as I was numb with fear, a fear I never felt before and hope to never feel again. I just needed to gather my thoughts, to block out everything outside my ultimate goal of reaching home. The bus moved slowly across the bridge. Other vehicles were filled with passengers. Some with expressions of fear on their faces, as did we. When the bus reached the center of the bridge, all eyes turned to look at the now altered skyline. Once again, the tears began to flow, and I sensed loss. I wondered about my friends, my co-workers, those on the trains at the time, those disembarking under the Trade Center. "Oh God, I can't think about that now," I whispered to myself. The bus was now edging its way to the toll plaza, and I had a sense of peace, as I was on the ground again and I was so close to reaching them, my family, my children. I tried the phone again to no avail. I started to think about where to go from here, since this bus would not take me anywhere near my home on the South Shore of the Island. I knew I could take another bus somewhere near to it, but I needed to get home soon, so I decided to get off the bus at the Grasmere Train Station. There, I could connect to the train which would bring me within blocks of my home. I needed to control myself from the pain I was feeling, the fear I felt all around me, and I needed someone to shelter me right now.

With the little bit of strength left in my body, I rang the bell to exit at the train station. I was the only person getting off at that stop. I waited for the cars to pass and slowly crept across the street in between traffic, and then to the train station. If I could move my feet, I would have walked the ten blocks to my husband's job, but I realized I could not and just headed toward the train. As I approached the station, I saw a young girl having a cigarette when it dawned on me it was eight hours since I had one. If I had not been in better shape, I should have stopped right then and there. However, my nerves were shattered and my body was still shaking, and I did not need an excuse for asking this young girl if I could have one of her cigarettes. It had been a lifetime since I grubbed a cigarette. I asked the young girl if I could have one of hers. She looked at me and asked, "Were you in the city when the planes crashed?" I responded with a faint, "Yes." She quickly reached in her bag and handed me a cigarette. She asked me many questions, although I was not listening, as I just puffed on the cigarette as though it was going to give me comfort. It didn't. I thanked her and proceeded down the staircase. When I got on the train, I saw so many people also coming from the tragedy and figured they had reopened the ferry. I sat into a seat and reached for my cell phone. I dialed home and for the first time I heard a ringing on the other end. My son, Keith, answered the phone, echoing, "Mom, where are you?"

"I'm on the train, and I will arrive in Huguenot in about ten minutes," I said. "Please be there for me." I hung up exhausted and dialed the phone again to reach Grandma. She answered crying. "Oh, I'm so glad you are okay," she uttered. "Call me when you reach home." I then just sat back in the seat and looked out at the surrounding blue sky and began to cry. I did not want to draw attention to myself so I tried desperately to control my emotions one more time. I looked out as the train moved along and realized that Staten Island still had blue skies. It appeared that the tragedy that occurred in Manhattan had not altered the island on which I lived. At each station, I heard the conductor calling out the stations by name, and the final leg seemed to take forever. I could not wait until I heard him echo the word, Huguenot. As I disembarked, dragging my feet, I held the railing to climb the three flights of stairs to the street level. There before me about two steps from the top, stood my son, Keith, and my daughter-in-law, Vikki. I looked at Keith and fell into his arms. I began to cry hysterically as we headed to the car. He dropped Vikki off at my vehicle, so she could drive it home, and we continued to the house. I cried like a baby, and I felt a little ashamed, but the time had now reached five-thirty in the evening, and I had restrained my emotions for long enough. He said nothing to me on the way home, but he comforted me as he rubbed my back with one hand and kept one hand on the steering column. I needed to speak no words, and for the first time in my life, I didn't.

As he pulled in the driveway, I could hardly believe my eyes. *Was I really home? Did I finally achieve the task of escaping death and reaching my destination?* I just entered the house and collapsed on the den couch. He ran to get me a blanket and I reached to turn the television on. He said, "Mom, watch it later." I couldn't help myself. I had to see for myself what I had escaped from. The screen lit up and I once again started to cry. I could not believe the devastation that I saw. I heard that possibly ten thousand people died, that firemen and police were trapped, and hundreds of people were still trying to flee the area. Then to my dismay, I heard that the planes belonged to us. Not only were there two planes, but that one crashed in Pennsylvania and one struck the Pentagon in Washington. *Oh my God, we are all going to die*, I thought, and still trying to keep calm. My son turned the television off, and I turned it back on and for the next forty eight hours I never moved from that spot. My husband just held me and told me to sleep.

"Sleep?" I responded. "How can I sleep?" I need to be awake in case it happens again, and I need to protect my family, but how was I going to do that when I could not even protect myself. *Help me, someone, I feel like I am falling and can't get up!*

Chapter Eleven

The Morning After

I must have fallen asleep a hundred times but each time I saw planes crashing, people jumping or myself running and running. Each time I awoke, I would turn on Channel 10, CNN News without hesitation. No wonder I could not sleep, the news was worse each time. Those poor firemen and policemen, I watched them the prior day as they rushed into the towers in hopes of saving lives and now I watch how their lives were lost. Those poor families who are being notified of their losses, the faces of many searching for their loved ones, my heart was aching for them. My thoughts of them were strong and I wrote a poem to let them know how horrible it truly was that they lost their lives helping others.

On Angel's Wings

Where oh where has the time flown to?
Where or when will I again see you?
You flew that day on an angel's wings
My sorrow grows but heaven sings

Where oh where have the people gone?
Why oh why, would they cause such harm?
Bring them back, from the wings of the dove
Bring them home to God who waits above

Why oh why, would you take from me?
Dear Lord, can you try to set me free
From the sorrow I know, the pain I feel
When dear lord will my heart start to heal?

Walk and walk, on the road side by side,
Help me to whisper those words of goodbye
When my turn comes to join him in heaven
That will end the pain of September Eleventh

Sadly, I now realized this was no dream—it was as real as real gets. I actually lived this horror and it seemed to only be getting worse. Helicopters and planes were flying low overhead, as my nerves started to rattle and I raised the volume on the television to drown out the noises above. The fear continued and it showed in the following poem that I wrote during my heavy medication period. The fear was there even then.

January 14, 2002

Realization of Fear

Fear is natural in life-threatening situations
It changes your life and your future expectations
It hurts a lot when loud noises surround you
When there is no one near to help you get through

It frightens me still to go in high places
I begin to panic and my heart starts racing
These fears are all real, they are there every day
Nothing one says, can take the fears away

Even now when it seems we are safe,
The slightest threat makes my head ache
Will I ever be ready to once again endure?
Will the day ever come when I will feel secure?

The terrorists have stripped me of all of my pride
Each time an alert is issued I become mystified
The lights from heaven gleam down through the night
But will it ever bring back the happy morning light

I had so many hopes, I had so many dreams
I always pictured my life flowing like a stream
Where are the answers, are they here on earth?
Will it take more than prayer to foresee a new birth?

I wonder, I pray, I try to find the aide
But there is no sunlight, I live in the shade
Only God can help expend the blooms in vain
Shelter me, my dear lord, covet me in the rain

Someday maybe I'll watch the buds on the trees
I'll stroll along the beach and feel the soft breeze
The truth of the matter lies deep within my mind
I just can't explain it, it's unjustly undefined

I tried to remember the trip home, but I was unable to visualize anything after the Manhattan Bridge. I know I was on Flatbush Avenue and Livingston Street but I can't remember what was there, only Third Avenue kept coming to mind.

A plane went overhead and I began screaming, as I ran to the basement because I feared it was about to strike something again. My husband stayed home that day to keep an eye on me, when he witnessed this episode, he called our family physician. The doctor recommended taking 20 mg of Paxil to keep me under some kind of control. A little later that day, my boss called to find out how I was doing. Being such a strong-willed person, the last thing I wanted him to know was that I was slowly coming apart. I told him I needed sleep and needed to try and keep away from the television, which kept reminding me of the vast reports of the horrors of what took place only twenty-four hours earlier.

The next morning my oldest son decided to help out and cut the lawn. When he turned on that lawn mower without my knowledge, he took ten more years off my life. It appeared that any engine noises were triggering some sort of reaction in my brain. It would be weeks after that until I could bear any loud noises.

After Brian had calmed me down, I could see sadness in his face. Thinking the worst, I asked him to tell me what was wrong. He informed me that his good friend, Craig Cannizzaro, had a brother missing in the Twin Towers. He was a fireman who rushed into save lives that day and now they feared he was gone. Craig was a great friend to my son all through high school and his brother was one of the funniest people my Brian said he had ever met. They probably hit it off real well since they shared the same first name. Craig's family was in shock over this tragedy, especially his wife and small son. Craig, himself, was devastated. How can you lose a brother? He was not prepared nor did I think he would ever be. A few months later Craig signed up to be a New York City firefighter. He is presently training and, although time has passed, the pain will not. I wrote the following to try and assure Craig that Brian will always be with him. He may not see him but he will always feel his presence. I never knew if it helped or not but I wanted him to know that I cared.

December 11, 2001
(It Has Been Three Months)

The Tears In My Eyes
(For Brian From Craig Cannizzaro)

Walk with me and talk with me
Let me feel you at my side
Stand by me when I fall down
And hold me when I cry
Tell me someday, it will be okay
Tell me someday I'll find a way
Of forgetting the pain, forgetting the tears
Will I ever forget, the memories of the years?
Walk with me and talk with me
I feel you by my side
Stand by me if I again fall down,
Wipe away my teardrops when I cry
Tell me lord he's happy with you on heaven's shore
Tell me he will be happy with you for evermore
You were in his heart here on earth
He loved you so much, it didn't hurt
Walk with me and talk with me
You are now closer by my side
It's better now, I won't fall down
Although the tears still fill my eyes
My brother, you are forever in my heart
And forever that's where you'll stay
I'll remember you like no one could
And I will feel your love every day

It was now Thursday morning, two days after the terrorist attacks. I could not control the sleeping habits I had. I was awake all night and slept in intervals during the day. I walked with my head down, afraid for anyone to see the pain in my face. I truly wanted to be strong for my family so I struggled whenever they were around to act in control of myself. I received word that my son Daniel, who attended college in Maryland, left the college at the onset of the attacks but was unable to reach Staten Island due to the lock down that was still in effect. He was hoping to reach home today from my brother's home in Iselin, New Jersey. I could not conceive of the lives I had affected by choosing to work in New York. If I had not worked in New York, my family would not be in such disarray. I had to put on a good act in front of Daniel, because he was the one who could read my mind, feel my heart. He arrived shortly thereafter and ran into the house hugging me. He said that, as he drove up the New Jersey Turnpike, he became aware that he would be unable to reach Staten Island anytime soon. "It was the worst drive I ever had," he revealed, "and I never want to be on the turnpike again." He described his emotions when he reached near to New York witnessing the normal city skyline filled with smoke and the unfortunate situation that he was unable to come home due to the closure of New York City and its surrounding boroughs. I could see the devastation in his face realizing that within forty miles of both his home and his college, attacks on our country took place. I needed to console him, and in doing so, I needed to reach into my heart and mind and forget the horror that I had been through. I had to put aside my fears in order to assure him his fears were not warranted and that at no time did I feel I was going to die. Maybe I needed this boost in order for me to believe that what I was saying was true. Is it wrong to lie to someone you love so deeply to ease their pain? I knew at that moment he needed to hear that I was okay and ready to return to my job, although I was going to be in Sheepshead Bay, Brooklyn for at least two months, at least that's what I was told. I decided to jot down my thoughts each evening when

I returned from work in Sheepshead Bay, Brooklyn. Our new work place was short-lived because, while I was on vacation, I received a call that I would be returning to Ground Zero on October 2nd. I was so frightened, but unable to show my fears to my employer, although they read my feelings in the first poem I wrote after our country's tragedy.

September 27, 2001

Will I Ever Forget?

Here I sit a mere three weeks later
Wondering when I will get it together
The fear, the horror, the lives I saw lost
No one can put a price on what this has cost

People ask where were you? Tower one, tower two
Did you see the planes, did you feel their pain?
Could you run, could you hide, did the tears fill your eyes?
Will you forget, oh not yet? Maybe someday if I try

The sadness, the tears, the search continues
Many are watching their hopes and dreams dwindle,
The funerals, the memorials, how can this be real?
How cruel of these people, will our hearts ever heal?

Our family is in pain, we are aware of at least nine,
Their lives are gone, three weeks ago they were fine
The fireman, the police, those who rushed to our side,
Now we must wish all of them, a sorrowful goodbye

Their families are shattered lonely and confused
Is this, our faith, how many more can we lose?
How does a day that began sunny and bright
Bring so much pain as the day turned to night

Where are the answers, I have searched everywhere?
Still I'm dazed, so confused, lonely and scared
I kneel before God, not sure what to say
Thanks for my life, is that what I pray?

The roar of those planes still with me each night
Watching them strike, then gone from sight,
Keep the evil ones away from heaven's door
Or our dreams of salvation will be never more

I look for your guidance to help me get through
I know I can't do it, at least not without you
Help me to comfort the families and friends
Convince my heart that the pain will soon end

Please bring us peace, a new way of living,
Make us believe that life is still, worth living
I look forward to the future and someday in heaven
I hope to forget the events, of September Eleventh

My one boss shook his head as it appeared he was sympathizing with me until I overheard him a few days later on the phone telling someone how he had been there and escaped safely. He was telling my story to whomever was on the phone. I felt betrayed, and for the first time, realized there were people that wanted to have a story to tell about that day, even if they didn't have one. I guess they would just tell the sadness of another's trials of that day.

Chapter Twelve

The Following Days

The next few days found me with continued strong feelings of fear, anxiety and desperation. I still could see the horror vividly each time I saw the planes strike the towers, and to this day, I shutter when a plane flies low. I could not get out of my mind the fact that our government could and did permit this act upon our nation and not be able to have prior knowledge of it. How does a group of terrorists hijack four aircrafts under our noses and reach their destination before anyone could do anything to prevent this horrific horror we all witnessed? Is anybody curious as to why this happened in a country where we have always been reassured that our safety was never in question? This was not an earthquake. It was sheer terror brought on by suicide bombers using our planes as their weapons. Where were our government officials? Was anyone watching the fort, the skies, the towers, the people? The following poem seemed to flow into my mind.

July 1, 2002

What Government?

No government to government, agency to agency
The FBI and CIA treat us as though we are crazy
Their lack of communications led to September 11th
What is it going to take to bring us back together?
The warning indicates that our protection level is five per cent
How could we feel safe, they ignored a serious request
Why should we put our faith into those who cannot heed
And yet they beg of us to continue in them to believe
So dear Mr. President and those who lead this world
How will you protect, can you help before we fall
Please don't ask the people to put their trust in you
When you know your confusion will never see us through
Wouldn't it be better to tell us what we should fear
Or do you think the danger will never reach us here
The polls say differently, we are due for another attack
Where are these terrorists and is our government coming back?

Many of the people being interviewed on the television questioned how God could permit such an extreme loss of life. I never blamed God, actually I praised him for my survival. In the beginning, as the funerals and memorials began to be announced, I felt ashamed to face my friends in their time of loss because I survived. Why did that make me feel so guilty? I had strong convictions about it for months following and it probably was at least eight to ten weeks later that I was able to sit down and write notes to them to follow up on their grief. This was a poem I shared.

October 8, 2001

Feeling Their Pain

Where do I begin, to tell you I feel your pain?
How can I possibly assure you they didn't die in vain?
The lives lost in the towers, the men who tried to save
The heroes we will honor, our flag remains to wave
I never knew true terror, I cannot believe I ran
This is my country and united we must stand
I try to forget what I was feeling on that sad, scarey day
Many dreams, hopes, and realities suddenly slipped away
Consoling each other is difficult as the tears flow
I understand the sadness more than you'll ever know
If I had known I could have switched places
I'd be gone but you would have smiling faces
I know my life was spared, only God can tell you why,
I sit, I stand, I lay, I walk, and yet I continue to cry
If only I could turn back time and make those towers stand,
Only then would it be easier for me to hold your hand.

My psychologist tried to explain that guilt was a normal reaction, especially when I needed to face those whose loss was so painful. Had this doctor not come to me when she did, I don't know if I would be where I am today. Her compassion was strong and she was a strong woman because many of the survivors had been her patients. I wrote this for her one morning on my way to my scheduled appointment. I think that was an emotional time for her, to truly know that she helped to return me to the land of the living.

July 15, 2002

She Was There

I was lost, alone and afraid
Into my life Dr. Seddio came
She looked at me and promised this
That the rest of my life I would not miss

She shared my pain, my tears, some joy
She treated me like a fragile toy
She heard, she felt, her heart was heavy
She knew my memories, she would have to bury

I shared with her the horrors of that day
She always looked at me in a special way
I knew I could trust her, she really did care
The pain I was feeling she wanted to share

Six months went by and still I couldn't smile
She told me sometimes it may take awhile
I wondered would I ever be the same
I felt betrayed, who should I blame?

Each day that passes I want to be me
I want to walk and feel my spirits free
But each time I hear a plane up in the sky
I wondered will this be my last goodbye

She gave me strength to walk with my fears
She even shared in my continuous tears
She made me believe that someday I'll soar
It would not had happened nine months before

I gave my faith to God and he gave me Dr. Seddio
Most people believe, I am much better you know
I am still afraid, but then aren't we all
With her in my life I believe I won't fall

So thanks for your time, your mind, your heart
You were so sincere right from the start
I attribute my improvements because you were there
Thank you for assuring me that God is still near

During those first few weeks, the memorials began for those found and murdered at the World Trade Center. With no explanation, as to how and why this all happened, it was a difficult time for those left behind. I can vividly see the pain in their eyes, and the gathering of thousands for each service brought little comfort. While a few chose to speak, most cried and others consoled another. The firemen looked dazed as they would daily line up along the churches to give a solemn farewell to their fallen comrades. How painful for them, when days before they were doing the normal tours of duty and now there was no time for rest. I can remember standing at Vesey and Church Streets, watching hundreds of them running into the building. The firemen were probably wondering, like I was, about how were they going to reach the people on the upper floors. A helicopter had been hovering over Tower One in an attempt to reach those who fled to the roof but to no avail. The smoke was billowing so high, the helicopter just could not get close enough to try a rescue attempt. When the second plane struck Tower Two it appeared the helicopter just disappeared into the fireball. I was later informed that the helicopter did escape the inferno. Now we had two burning buildings. I have often said that the first plane seemed to have shut the engines down before striking, and that is what caught the attention of many because the noise was incredibly loud. The debris that came off the building was amazing. People started to scream and yell, and I think we all realized at that precise moment that New York City was under attack. Still I watched those brave firemen continue to take their equipment and rush into the burning buildings and do what they did best, save lives. Immediately following, a black car came down Vesey Street in the wrong direction and when it reached the corner of Church Street, our infamous mayor Rudolph Guiliani emerged with shock and disbelief. He was surrounded by security and ushered off to the towers on Vesey and Church Streets. Soon after that I began to run in the opposite direction toward Broadway. The people that were on the south side of Church Street were being directed to West Street and we were advised to head north. *North to the river*, will always echo in my mind. Each time I took a second to glance back, the horror was worst. Metal was flying, and the vicinity was totally covered in layers of office paper which must have been blown from the upper levels now laid in piles on the ground. The police department kept some officers with us, keeping us moving at a quick pace. As we tried to clear the area, my thoughts immediately went back to the towers, as I traveled with so many people that worked in there. *How many got out?* I asked silently to myself.

Immediately after, I began with the feeling of guilt. How could I have been so lucky, while these poor, innocent people who ventured to New York each morning from all walks of life are now dead? Why would anyone be so vicious to harm the working Americans? Well, the answer immediately came to me. They wanted to hurt our economy and what better way to accomplish this than to shut down the Financial District. Later than evening I watched what I had etched in my mind for the past forty-eight hours, with my heart breaking for those brave firefighters, policemen, rescue workers and port authority workers, who so valiantly gave their lives for others. I could not deal with myself for running away instead of trying to at least do something to save someone. So the guilt continued on with me for weeks, then months, and I told myself that, had I been stronger, maybe one more life would have been saved. But I did not go back. I just continued running to the river!

Chapter Thirteen

A Friend's Pain

A neighbor on our street lost her son, a young twenty-nine-year-old. He had just become a stock broker that day at a big breakfast meeting. He was on the 92nd floor of Tower One. We knew from the beginning that he was gone, although we continued to pray. It was hard to know the outcome was going to be dramatically sad. His name was Mark Petrocelli. He was young, ambitious and had a wife of two years. My son Brian grew up on the street with Mark from the time they were learning to ride their big wheels. It was a type of ride on truck that sounded like a hundred bowling balls coming down the street. I kept in touch with his mom often although she is nowhere near ready to share in the grief that she is suffering with. I wrote a poem for them of our memories of Mark. I wanted them to know I could feel their pain.

September 29, 2001

Our Friend "Mark Petrocelli"

You are gone but our memories are vivid,
The pain of losing you has left us all livid
Bright young and happy, married and carefree
You had it all, it was there for all to see

I saw mom, dad, Albert and gave a hug to nicole
I thought I would watch the two of you grow old
But faith had a way of changing my view
Sadness, tears and loneliness took the place of you

How I wish I could turn back the hands of time
Take away the evil, make all peoples kind,
Your body is gone but your soul flies free
Thank God we all cherish a special memory

God blesses you in heaven, as an angel you will see
A new way of living for your family and for me
When I look to the skies as you soar with all your might
I will be comforted that an angel is near us day and night

I remember my friend and his mother, Ginger, telling me she planned to frame it. It is still difficult to face her. I try but as soon as I sense her withdrawal, I once again become reluctant to try again. To this day, we seem to talk about everything and yet nothing because the wounds will never heal. I know it and I know she knows it too. Her life remains to be a group of empty, unanswered questions, while she worries of the uncertain future for her young, widowed daughter-in-law. Wanting to comfort her husband in this time of sadness and yet needing to be comforted herself is more than one person can bare. How does a mom let go? Under normal circumstances, it is difficult. Under this tragic circumstance, it's impossible! I want to say so much to her but what right do I have to comfort her? And I feel that I'm a reminder that others survived, as she again questions, why did her son die? Did God have this planned? Was it God's will? Or, was He also unable to stop the terrorists and change the course of history? Was it God's will to take an angel and give him wings, a sacrifice for those left behind, and yet their faith in God is still unshaken? I know she continues to question how such a tragedy could happen and yet she knows there will never be a true understanding of any of it. If she is angry, she conceals it, but her tears are just not as easy to conceal. I believe that God was there that day, but the terrorists had such a determined will to destroy that it blocked God's intercession. His angels struggled to assist, and I'm sure many received their wings that day. Why should we not question where our government was? This was its responsibility and yet it failed to protect. Were our officials telling us the whole truth or just enough to keep us calm? Now in the present, we know that not only was our president aware of the impending threat, but also that he decided not to panic the people. After all, it is always more important to keep the economy intact instead of protecting those that work to improve it. We now know that had they given us a warning of an impending attack, more of the people in the towers would have reacted differently, and they would have known immediately that our country was in danger. There would not have been any hesitation in evacuating the building, the police would have not directed others to return to Tower Two, the firemen would not have entered so quickly and the majority of the people would have reacted more quickly and decisively. Ultimately the death toll would have been much lower. But that was yesterday and now we wonder if the next time will be a different scenario.

Last Sunday was Mother's Day. I knew in my heart that I would not be able to celebrate with my family without sharing in Ginger's pain. I went to the florist and purchased a bouquet of all white flowers to bring to her. When I phoned to be sure I could stop in, I knew it was probably the worst day yet for her. I knocked on the door and gave her a hug that I wanted her to know was from my heart. Her demeanor was quiet yet welcoming even in the pain she was feeling. She has always been a gracious and compassionate woman. As I walked back to my home, I cried for her, I felt her pain, well not really; only she could feel that kind of pain. So I wrote about Mother's Day.

May 10, 2002

A Mother's Wishes

Today is Mother's Day, for me it will be fun
Sharing the day with thoughts of my three sons
Invited for dinner by Brian and his wife
It seems as though things are right in life

I was brought many flowers and twenty-four roses
It signifies my happy life, photos without poses
Never again will I feel so alone or aloof
For today those who love me provided the proof

Not that I needed reassurance, though it does tell
That priorities in my life are simply going well
My day was as free as the flight of birds
I want to hear each of them utter those words

Mom you did well, we all turned out okay
That is what I heard from them today
I pray that with my deeds I have truly inspired
To give them what is needed and always required

Required to live in a world with no room for failing
With true ambition and many memories recalling
Thank you for making my day bright and blue
I really do love and care for the four of you

Now we go forward! How is that possible? The threats continue and yet the government continues to issue warnings, high alert, low alert, too late alert. Why does a person not have the same worth as the businesses they are employed by? Do we ever come to trust our government again? Can we trust that they will issue warnings? Or will we again be made to suffer through terror for profit? I knew from that first day that the government was covering up a lot of information. Why not be honest to your people? The bible does state that when the time nears for God to return, there will be deceit between the people and their representatives. He knew thousands of years ago, that money would be the evil of the world. Protect the financial institutions and worry not about mankind. How does my neighbor struggle to understand that these statements are true? Why would any of us trust them again? Last week, they issued a warning for a future attack for July 4th. Today, May 20th, we are told that the concern for another terrorist attack on the United States is not a matter of "if" but "when." It could happen today, next week, next month. Threats on apartment buildings, Walt Disney World, nuclear plants, etc. Again, we will alter our lives. We use to feel safe living in a free environment. So again, we must decide individually whether we want to stay close to home or attempt to live our lives as we did prior to September 11th. I wrote this on the ferry yesterday when the boat stopped out in the bay for an unknown reason.

May 19, 2002

Alert In New York Again

While sitting in the peace of the beach and ocean
CNN announced New York had more commotion
Each time I think I can once again feel free,
Today, they threatened the Statute of Liberty

Once again my heart raced back to that day
When the towers came down and the skies turned gray
The day my mind just responded with why?
Again I will tremble when I look to the skies

I look up to reassure myself that He is still there
That He will be listening to my endless prayers
I think back to when the towers fell like sticks
The sign He left was the free standing crucifix

I called home and told them I'm afraid to come back
Bloomberg said that's 'exactly how they want you to react
Easy for him when in ten minutes he'll jump on a jet
Giuliani come back and let him know it's hard to forget

Compassionate he is not, I tried to give him a chance
Does he ever question the hurt and the circumstance?
Do you think of the families that listen to your reports?
Do you ever think about their pain and their tragic lost?

Sometimes people say things that are not very polite
I relive September 11ᵗʰ when I try to sleep every night
Someday you may have to speak with the fatherless kids
But until then Mr. Mayor, meet us on the Brooklyn Bridge

Staten Island Advance

950 FINGERBOARD ROAD • STATEN ISLAND, N.Y. 10305 • TEL (718) 981-1234

1/22/03

Here's your signed copy —
and personalized to boot!
Give me a call —

Barbara

Although I am not in the poor state of mind as I had been, I still worry about my family and friends. I question all plans on where my life should go, where my heart will go, who do I turn to, other than God, because as you are probably aware, prayers are heard, government requests are denied. The saying on all our currency reminds us of those infamous words, "In God We Trust." Little did any of us know how important those few words would be and will be as we move forward to the future. Did our government actually realize a hundred years ago that money would be the downfall of our country? Did our forefathers have insight into where it would take us down the road? We can question all we want but the answers are obviously no where to be found. I believe our government owes all Americans an apology for acting in a monetary manner when it came to the safety of the human life not just in New York and Washington, D.C., but the entire country, for we all suffered in one way or the other because of the tragedy.

On August 10th, 2002, Mark Petrocelli was laid to rest at Resurrection Cemetery in Staten Island. I knew I had to go and share in the possible closure for our friends Ginger and Al and for Mark's wife, Nicole and his brother Albert. The tears flowed as if it were yesterday, their sorrow written all over their faces, the loss of a husband, son, brother, a loss that had finally brought them here today in the open fields where I once played on the grounds of Mount Loretto. I looked around and thought what a perfect spot for Mark, he will be in the middle of everyone when the cemetery is full. As he was in life the center of his family and friends, his final resting place will follow in the same path. I hugged Ginger, Al and his brother but never had the opportunity to express my condolences to Nicole because she never moved a step from in front of the grave. I guess she knew in her heart that Mark was finally at rest and she wanted to watch him sleep for a short while. If he could have spoke to her he would have uttered these words.

November 8, 2001

My Last September
(Mark's Words)

Septembers come and Septembers go
The pain this September you could never know
The screeching sounds of engines so loud
Little did we know of the approaching cloud

We saw them run to the river, don't follow me,
No, don't stop, there is no time to see,
Run to the river, if you want to survive
Run to the river and close your eyes

The clouds are so thick, where did everyone go?
Lord this is the time I need to let you know
Tell my family I love them, tell them I was brave
Tell them I'll be watching, tell them I was saved

The smoke is overpowering, I felt no pain over me
Lord, this is the time I need to let you see
Tell her she was always my life and my pride
Tell her she was the most elegant beautiful bride

It's time to meet the angels, I see the ray of light
Oh it is so peaceful watching the angels in flight
Tell the world it's beautiful, I did not die in vain
Tell the world I'm home now, heaven has no pain

Chapter Fourteen

Survivor

Survivor guilt is becoming a common trend. Many of us need to become productive human beings again. I was fired because I was afraid, afraid of unchartered waters, unchartered skies so deep into the core. I worked not a hundred feet from the corner of the attack. I was unable to face that horror by returning so soon after the attack. I truly believed, had my company stayed in Brooklyn, then my mental state would have remained intact. It was watching the clean up, the smell, the crying families and the Ground Zero area surrounded by cops, firemen, national guardsmen, it was like watching a movie, yet it was no movie, no ending.

Post Traumatic Stress Syndrome has affected more than 100,000 people and continues to mount even now after eight months. Statistics say more and more people, firefighters, and your average workers have developed fear factors that require drug treatment and stress therapy.

Two people could have seen and experienced the same disaster yet both react differently. When I asked my therapist why, she said a lot would go back to the way one was raised, by whom, and how many fears one had prior to the terrorist attack. Those who were as close to the devastation as I was, witnessed the deaths of those who choose to jump rather than face the reality of burning in the towers or falling with them. I know that as one who witnessed those deaths, I will never be able to comprehend the feelings of those people or being in a position to make a choice so unbelievable, yet so definitive.

My parish of Our Lady Star of the Sea and Pastor Jeff Conway had the job of memorializing and burying a multitude of parishioners. I can vaguely remember the services, but at least I remember being there for those that I knew. The job of having to console so many families must have taken a toll on the Pastor. How sad that we lost such good caring people, most of them were firemen. Once again, I must mention that it was difficult to walk up to the families and give my condolences when I felt they were staring at me and wondering why I was there and their lost loved one was gone. Yes, I survived that horrific day and I know as long as I live, I will never forget. Not one American should ever forget what was done to us on our own soil. In the years to come we must never forget those widows, orphans or parents who lost loves of their life. We need to stand behind them in their decision on the future of the area referred to as "Ground Zero." After all, it is part of their lives that ended there, their loved ones who rest there and they are the people that should have the right to a say in the matter. Be there for those you know, hug them, listen to them, for their sorrow is not over, nor will it ever be.

Because of the period of time that I was heavily medicated I must admit I can see how people become addicted to drugs. Why not put yourself in a stupor and life will pass you by? You don't have to think, worry, respond or even answer when questions are asked of you. I know, after October 3rd when my company let me go, it was as though my brain could take no more. The following day my medication was upgraded to the following doses; 20 mg of Paxil, 20 mg of Xanax (a demoralizing drug) and Ambien, which is a sleeping pill. It is no wonder that my blackout time lasted until October 25th. I have no memory of anything during that period.

My husband had what they thought was a heart attack. It was a blockage to the arteries which required the insertion of a pace maker. I have no recollection of this ordeal and yet I am told I was there through it all. I am sure that frightens you, because it frightened me dramatically. So many days of my life were stripped from me because of the terrorists. Days that I will never get back, and obviously I will never remember them. I haven't to date and it appears that my brain chose to put it in the back room for safe keeping. I try so hard to remember but there is nothing. I knew I would never take this Xanax again. Besides losing my job to uncompassionate employers, I could have lost myself to the Xanax.

I knew I was too strong to have continued into oblivion. I wrote a few poems during that period that probably explain what I was feeling.

October 25, 2001

Coming Back Stronger

The medication was causing my mind not to function
I decided it was time to move onto a new junction
I woke up today and realized there are no guarantees
But I will follow God, my only warranty

For weeks I have hidden like an exhausted lion
Existing in this life without really trying
But today I am determined to become like before
Watch me world, I'm coming back with a roar

I won't live like a slave in this country again
I end all my prayers to God with a determined amen
Surely I know I can turn uncertainty into hope
I will challenge myself and I will learn to cope

Today, I start to change my mind through my heart
I'm convinced it will be an amazing new start
I now look to the skies and I can fall to my knees
Never will a terrorist cause my life to freeze

I'm still mending, today I walked on the sand
I walked with my husband, quietly, hand in hand
The peace, the tranquility, the waves on the shore
A day I finally wanted to remember for evermore

October 26, 2001

A New Day Is Dawning

Today I woke up determined to stand erect
I need it for myself, an example I can set
Learning to control my mind with meditation
Has aroused my desire for mental relaxation

I decided that my career truly bores me
Now I'm left with a lack of security
But it's not new, this person full of strife
Will I eventually learn, to enjoy a new life?

Wishing and hoping is two different things
It is my hope that I will struggle and win
With laughter, understanding and friends so kind
So many reasons to change my frame of mind

The medications have eased anxiety and stress
Now it is time to straighten out this mess,
I suffered, succumbed, now my strength is back
Never again will I allow this invasive attack

Chapter Fifteen

The Learning Years

As the children began to grow older, we continued to live in our quiet three bedroom home only two miles from the "Mount" where Pat and I first met. We would often pass the Mount on our way to the Little League fields in Tottenville. All of the boys were sports oriented. In the spring and summer it was baseball and during the fall and winter it was basketball. We kept them busy with an array of organizations and thus kept them off the streets. I remember telling Brian, the oldest, "You will drive a car on Amboy Road before you ride a bike on it." Little did I know that my fib would come true. My husband and I spent six non-consecutive years on the sports committee at Our Lady Star of the Sea School. This entailed all our weekends for the fall and winter. When we would have a scheduled day off, we would spend it visiting family. Sports was a diversion from the streets but our family was always important. My brother had two sons close in age with Daniel and Keith. They grew up more like brothers. They enjoyed each other's company and my brother and I couldn't have been happier. They danced, laughed, bowled, had vacations in the Poconos and Ocean City, Maryland. Every page of our photo albums shows Adam and Shaun beside their cousins. The hundreds of albums of pictures show a lifetime of memories, five kids who stuck together through it all. If one had a problem, they all had the problem.

Like all other families, we had our problems too. It seemed like every day was another challenge. When I look back now, I know without a doubt that I would do it all over again if I had the chance. I'm sure I would leave out September 11th, 2001. The years passed and sending three children to private school through the twelfth grade is quite costly. I worked my entire life to pave a way for them to become the moral men they are today. College was actually more reasonable since Brian chose the community college on Staten Island. When Daniel was ready for college, he knew he was going away. We researched all schools that excelled in communication arts since Daniel always wanted to be a sports broadcaster. He chose to attend Salisbury University in Maryland. Keith also chose to attend the community college on Staten Island.

I knew at this time that, in order to keep up with an eighteen-thousand-dollar-a-year tab on college tuition, I needed to head for New York. The first interview that I went on seemed to be exactly what I was looking for and vice-versa. I spent a good four years at this firm, although the ending of the relationship is hard to understand. The office was disorganized when I started there and the prior office manager was running her own business from their office. She had been running an immigration service within our office. Her dealings included bringing these people to the office at times when she knew the bosses were out on court cases. I never really paid much attention since the task of organizing this office took at least nine hours a day with a thirty minute break. I worked very hard, and being the perfectionist that I am, I did it right the first time to avoid redoing it again in the future. The system that this law office had was called the Saga System. If one had litigation experience the drafting of pleadings were simplified. When the system was installed, there was little training on it. I had been working on this system for six years and had no problem operating it to capacity. I began to teach the office staff on the value of utilizing all of the features that were offered with this system so it would make the work load lighter.

Once the bosses realized my ability and found out that the office manager was illegally doing immigration under their name, they arrived early one morning and fired her as she entered the premises. I should have known at the time that anyone who could be so callous to one employee would never hesitate in the future to treat others in the same manner. One morning, one of the bosses spilled his coffee on the desk. I quickly ran to grab paper towels and then helped him to clean off the desk. A part-time worker came in and told me that no one does anything for him except for her. I looked strangely at her and left his office. As I strolled down the corridor toward my office, I could hear the arguing going on between the two of them. Later that day I was approached by this same young seventeen-year-old and told that he was her man, her man and if anything needed to be done for him, she would do it. I told her where she could go and probably would be going there in the near future. It became quite apparent that this nice-looking attorney well into his thirties was having a relationship with this seventeen-year-old snot. As it turned out two months later, I was instructed to fire her because she was stalking him outside of the office. I always questioned who was stalking who after speaking to the building maintenance manager who informed me to be careful of my boss because shady things have been going on longer than I was aware of. I soon began to realize the truth of this when speaking with the other office employees who adamantly claimed he was sadistic and had mental problems when it came to young women. Not being into office gossip, I heeded their concern and let it go. During the following year, I had to let go of three more girls who had found their way to his office to look at pornographic sites on the Internet. Training people was not one of my stronger suits, and I was becoming quite frustrated in training and then having to let young girls be fired because of this attorney. I finally succumbed to the fact that the only way to avoid this situation from continuing was to try to hire some people that did not appeal to him. That is what

I finally did and yet the Internet porno continued on a daily basis. I am more than fifty and was down that road many times, so I just turned the other cheek and knew it was going to continue no matter what I did. And continue it did. He would take the younger girls out at night and never once consider the feelings of the three other women who did not become involved in his little games. I spent so much time trying to pacify the other employees. It started to affect my determined effort to make the office a quality law firm.

It was totally ironic that the other owners were never made aware of the problems related to this one attorney. When asked why they were let go, this attorney would say it just was not working out or he would tell them that they found a better job. I was beginning to realize that the honesty level in this office even among the owners was not what it had appeared to be on my interview. One boss who was rarely in the office, but whom I believed was the most decent of the three, should only know the truth behind all the firings and the continued animosity amongst the employees.

On October 3rd when I returned to the Vesey Street office, I shuttered at the sight and smell that surrounded me. I struggled throughout the day to tell myself that it will work out. I never considered leaving my job since I knew it well and needed to continue supporting my son at college. That day was very difficult for me. I decided to unpack the sixteen boxes that we brought back from the temporary office of a lawyer in Sheepshead Bay. He was a close friend of my boss, as they were law students together from what I understood. While unpacking, I suggested to one of the girls to grab a box and sort through it. Her response was simple. She said "That is not in my job description." This is what I dealt with concerning the young office females because of their relationship with the one attorney. If they did not like what I told them to do, they would run to him and instead of supporting his manager, he would tell them to "just ignore her." The mailman had arrived and the stack of mail was massive. I went back to my desk and spent an hour opening mail, and while my ankle was killing me,

I finished my job before leaving the office for the day. As I left the office, I bid a "goodnight" to the receptionist, and left for home. I was not sure where I was to catch the bus and upon leaving the office I began to cry, the harsh reality of the day had set in and I was mentally becoming undone. I ran into two employees out for lunch who came over and asked what had happened. I just responded that it was a hard day and I needed to escape this area, finding it very difficult to cope around the thousands who were still hoping to find survivors. When I returned home about four-thirty, I just laid down on the couch and thought about the events of the day. I grabbed some paper and wrote a poem about this day in New York.

October 3, 2001

Good Morning Heartache

Good morning New York, you are so beautiful but I'm afraid
It wasn't your fault that you suffered, it's not you that I blame
I fear for your safety and I know they want to bring you down
I'm sorry that when they do, I don't want to be around

I want more of my life, I choose to stand on solid ground
I know it sounds selfish but it's the answer I have found
Can you please forgive me, someday you will understand?
New York and I no longer can walk hand in hand

Constant threats, can the security protect your shores
Although you will be in my heart today and forever more
They say you can't take the life from a native New Yorker
But the terrorists are threatening us like vigilant stalkers

I have always worked to put my faith in God
But he can't be everywhere, for me only in my heart
He's telling me to move on, to be strong and be brave
Yet the question of where to turn is still my prime concern

They can close your bridges and block the tunnels to you
But knowing the terrorists they will still get through
They want to harm you because you stand so tall
Tall like the towers and yet they made them fall

New York is my home, to you I will always look
Though I need to find a stream with a running brook
Our government let us down, we know we were forsaken
Our hearts won't forget, if they think so, their mistaken

I'll pray for you, for the strength of all New York
So sorry that the road to you has developed into a fork
Keep our flag waving and this wish for you I make
Stay safe, we cannot bear another New York heartache

The next morning my husband contacted the receptionist to advise that I would not be coming in. He was told that the bosses had been mean to me the day before, when he questioned me about it, I truly did not remember any incident of them being mean. That night at approximately seven-thirty, the attorney adored by the porno group phoned my home and told me he had been informed that I had quit. I told him how ridiculous a statement that was, and I asked him, to whom did I give my notice to? He said that "it didn't matter. That it was best this way. We love you, we love your kids, stay home." At first, I looked into the phone with astonishment and then I realized he was not joking. I adamantly told him I did not quit, and he said it was better this way and hung up the phone. That is when my depression started to really kick in. The doctor prescribed additional medication called Xanax. The next day I remember is October 25th, and my first thought that day was, I was fired! Could this be real? Have I become a victim for the second time? As unbelievable as it may seem, it is certainly true. How could a person that you spent years buying coffee for, bringing apples to, baking cakes for and organizing all office functions and work, be so cruel to treat someone so shabbily? Where were the trust and loyalty? Money says it all. The firm owed me bonuses that kept getting put off until the next quarter, a raise that I had been waiting patiently for since the end of June, but never materialized. I guess they were just waiting for their opportunity and I gave it to them when I began suffering from the effects of the attacks on the World Trade Center.

I found it so hard to believe. I trusted these people. I did everything by the book. And if the one boss had an addiction to pornographic web sites, is this the reason I was let go? I tried hard to explain to my family that they were protecting me. I was beginning to believe this until they refused to have me back on the premises to retrieve my personal belongings. They would not return my phone calls nor did they ever try to contact me to discuss an obvious misunderstanding. Or, did they realize that they needed to save money during the following months? Whatever their reasoning, they were wrong? They should have had enough concern for me to help me through this rough time. Instead, they fought me for benefits from both unemployment and Workman's Compensation. This went on for ten months and finally I was awarded compensation after a third court hearing where the attorney for the insurance carrier advised the judge that the claim was no longer being controverted. The benefits that I should have been receiving from Workmen's Compensation and my unemployment were restored. What made this company act as it did? Was it intentional or just nervous anxiety on their part?

During the month of January, I decided to seek out new offers for a job. Staten Island had little to offer, so without hesitation, I doggedly admitted that I must return to New York. I needed to go to New York for employment not because of the difference in the money but for the knowledge I might forget because of my constant medication. Finally I answered an ad in the Staten Island Advance for a position with a law firm in downtown Manhattan near the Seaport. That day God must have been by my side for I met a group of people who would help to bring me back to New York and protect me. I truly believed after a few weeks with this firm that I would be the first they would remove from the building, their understanding of my trauma was so sincere, so compassionate, so kind. They made all the difference in the world to me. I felt protected, protected from the terrorists, protected from the memories and especially protected by God within this great company.

Chapter Sixteen

Trying To Move Forward

It has been quite sometime since I have felt safe. My company gave everyone July 4th and 5th off. They were very kind to let me switch my Tuesday to Monday which gave me a full week to try and finish this book. I worked all day, went home, picked up my dog and headed to the only tranquil place I have known since September 11th. As I headed over the Delaware Memorial Bridge with Peaches, my dog, sitting in the passenger seat, I felt that calm of peace come over me. Each time I glanced over at her, I could see the love and companionship we had in each other. I was sure that being out of New York gave me a sense of safety, yet I always think I could once again be in the wrong place at the wrong time. I opened the windows to the cool breeze and the stars filled skies. I turned on the Delilah show and listened to the music and stories of other people's problems, praises and beliefs. As I leisurely drove along Route 1 heading toward the shores of Ocean City, Maryland, I began to consider the possibilities which lie ahead. My one worry this July 4th holiday weekend was that my children would be attending the New York Yankee game at Yankee Stadium. It was a gift to my son for his graduation from college and he had invited his cousins Shaun and Adam and his brother, Keith. I could not get it off my mind that four of the six loves of my life would be in an open, densely populated, high-profile, public space for the holiday. Will I ever forget the fear I felt that September day? I can't help but feel that these terrorists have a new plan, just waiting for us to let our guard down. Please God I prayed, "let them be safe." I never again want to know the pain that so many felt when they lost their loves one on September 11th. I also thought about the people who tell me to move on, that it's over and threats can't hurt me. Although it seems like sound advice, they did not have to run for their life on that day. I can't get angry with them because they just don't understand that my fear was real, and that I felt trapped in a city that once had held so many happy times. So many thoughts were running through my head as I continued along the dark peaceful roadway leading to the Delmarva peninsula.

As I drove along the shore line with the moon roof open and the clear cool breeze sweeping over me, I tried to think of happier times. Sometimes I focused on the negative rather than strive to be positive. Before our tragedy, I was always a positive person with a great outlook on my future and continued accomplishments. I count my blessings for a great husband, three sons and a wonderful daughter-in-law. Yet, I find it difficult to enjoy them to the fullest because of the continued threats and alerts. I want them to know that they are the reason for my living. To have their love and their understanding makes all the strife bearable. They have put up with many moods and outbursts as I continue to wean myself off the medications. I think to myself how I spent my life raising them to enjoy their lives and now I was unable to follow my own advice. I then think—will they even have a life if these evil doers continue their quest to bring this country down? Will they raise their children in the freedom that I had known once upon a time? I would do anything to guarantee them that promising future. Then I think about how the government let us down. How could all these agencies have failed so terribly to protect the people of the United States? I wondered if I could ever again believe in anything that they say in the future. It has become obvious that their only concern is for the economy, and if we lose a few thousand people doing that, well that's the price we pay. I sat back in my seat and thought, *enough thinking about the things I have no control over*. As I continued the drive, I thought about the feeling of anxiety slowly dying away. The further I drove away from New York, the safer I felt.

I arrived at Ocean City at approximately nine-thirty p.m. I was excited to think that I had a whole week to enjoy the beauty of the ocean. Actually for the first time since the attack, I ventured the trip alone. Maybe it was a sign of better things to come. I stopped to take a look around and realized it truly is different here, that it's not just my imagination. Peaches was excited also as she jumped from the car to inspect any new scents that had developed during our absence. I unpacked and settled in for a week of relaxation, the kids were in New York with their dad and all seemed right with the world; at least the part of the world I was in.

The forecast promised to be hot, hazy and humid with temperatures well into the nineties. I needed some sunshine. I needed to just relax on the beach with my laptop and listen to the roar of the ocean, one of God's greatest wonders. The next morning it felt good to be alive as I headed for the beach nice and early. I sat back opened my laptop and began to sink into my beach chair. About five minutes into my solitude, a plane flew overhead. My first thought, of course, was to look up and see where it was headed. Finally, after ten months, I looked at this low flying aircraft without fear. It has been a long time since I did not look away from the roar of a plane. I was thrilled that for the first time since September 11th, I was capable of looking to the skies once again. Would this be the start of my healing process or did I just feel truly safe here in Maryland? The next plane flew by and I looked again. It finally dawned on me that I used to enjoy watching planes. Plane after plane passed by and I realized I finally could look up at them without fear. With each passing plane, I could feel myself having a renewed strength, a determined will to look to skies without the fear, a fear that has overshadowed me since September 11th. The only accomplishment I had left would be too once again fly on a plane.

Not likely to be accomplished at the present time. I had promised I would never fly again and yet maybe that will subside also. I hope so since I have a wedding in Denver on Columbus Day weekend and because of the close relationship between my girlfriend and I, after her rescuing me from Mount Loretto, I know I must be there that day for her. Her daughter plans to wed on the 12th of October to a nice young man named Justin. Besides, she flew to New York to be at my son's wedding three years ago. I must find the courage to board the plane.

One of the saddest thoughts is realizing that people are forgetting. It is July 4th, and here in Ocean City, flags are flying everywhere. The flags are on the cars, and on my car, but back in New York, we are back to the old way of complaining about the little things that are really so unimportant. Have New Yorkers found so much strength that they forgot how we all had come together and became better people, during the attacks? Why can't our world be like that every day? Can't we just learn to live together and work together without the racism that runs rampant in this country? Why can't people become people that God could be proud of, not just in times of trouble, but always? When I think back to my days in Mount Loretto, there were no color barriers. We never looked at each other as a color or race, we were all in the same boat and I have put a lot of effort in teaching my children to be the same way. My neighbors down in Ocean City, Maryland invited me to go with them to see the fireworks a few blocks away. I had to decline since I still cannot deal with crowded areas and loud noises are not on my agenda just yet. Their kindness was appreciated but some of us still need to avoid situations that make us feel anxious and frightened. I spent a few hours on the beach trying to gather my thoughts. I find I can accomplish that by listening to the waves hitting the shore and the laughter of small children being buried in the sand. It reminds me of my own children growing up and the hard work that goes into having a good family relationship. It is not always easy but the challenge is all worth it. I watched the families playing in the sand and the children crying when their sand castles were swept away with the tide. I related that to the destruction of the Twin Towers. All that hard work, all the people working together only to have it destroyed by the unforeseeable hatred that lingers all around us. I think often of the families directly affected and how they must feel when they see children who remind them of the ones they lost. A grandparent burying her child instead of the child burying the grandparent. So much pain, so much disbelief and the answers of how this happened still go unanswered in the minds of many.

Out in the distance, I can see a silver lining in the high clouds. Simple, beautiful sights as these, a ship traveling north can bring such horror if our country does not infiltrate the shipments that can cause more tragedy and pain. Where do we go from here and when we do go? Will our dreams once again for our children and their children again be realized? Can this country be taken over by these terrorists? What are their plans? How do we secure our ports and skies?

Unfortunately, this morning on CNN, they reported that our airports are not very secure. The announcer on the radio said he would not put his family on a plane for all the money he was offered. One in four people has slipped past security and boarded planes with guns, knives and paper cutters. He said he was told that at Newark International Airport they spot check fully every forty people. He was told of a group of sixty-year-old women headed for a school reunion that were pulled from the line. They had to remove their shoes and empty their belongings. While these so-called uneducated people are checking this innocent group of older women, killers could be boarding the planes with no one paying attention. The systems surely need to be revamped. I worry that if everyone begins to feel as I do, the airlines will suffer dramatically. The airlines will have to get more qualified educated people and not pay six dollars an hour to someone who does not care about the importance of their job. I worry that if everyone begins to feel as I do, the airlines will suffer dramatically. My thoughts went back to the day when I was forced to walk clear across Brooklyn, and I chuckled to myself as I thought that maybe I can just walk wherever I have to go. If I could walk through Brooklyn from

Manhattan, I can find ways to reach my other destinations without the use of planes. That was probably the last thing I remembered during that walk. I suppose by believing I could do it, I would do it. I do need to believe that I will fly again, but I never had fear before now. All things will come in its time. I sat back again in my chair and wrote the following:

4ᵗʰ of July

Today the country will celebrate a day known throughout history
A day that's a fact not fable, to none is it a mystery
People dressed in red, white and blue from their shirts to their shoes
And no one needs to read about it in the Times or the Daily News

What is news worthy is the fear that the day could bring
For the terrorists are threatening to hurt us once again
For me that is fearful, I am sorry that they get to me
But on September 11ᵗʰ they robbed me of my liberty

I sat here near the television, I guess I didn't know for sure
If their hatred for our country would once again reach our shore
They are the kind of people who don't care how many they kill,
To them they have little regard for life, to harm is just a thrill

I worried for my family, they stayed back in New York
I worried for myself, it's a fight I keep in my thoughts
As the night came and the darkness drew the crowds
I sat and said a prayer that God would not let them allow

An opportunity to harm us, I prayed to keep the United States safe
For I believe our country could not bear another disgrace
The damage of that day, the damage in our hearts and souls
Will be with us today and 'til the day our bodies turn cold

I looked to the north and watched the fireworks light the skies
An American Flag was the finale a reminder of past times
In my heart I remembered the World Trade Center flag as it once flew
And softly wiped tears from my eyes, and thought of those that I knew

The day is over and maybe now my fears will lessen
Knowing that God is beside me, gives me a feeling of special blessings
Just as I know that many others are feeling the way that I do
I'm proud to be an American, I stand by the red, white and blue

Chapter Seventeen

Tomorrow Is Another Day

I woke up early around six a.m. and rushed to the television to turn on CNN. I started this habit after the attack. I was so relieved that the only incident was at Los Angeles International Airport in California. They have not yet declared that it was an attempt by terrorists. I was relieved to know that the people in our country successfully celebrated July 4th without another incident by the so-called terrorists. They are playing with our emotions and maybe at this time our country has set up enough security to keep them at arms length. It is difficult for the free American to accept the threats of ruthless, heartless, people who believe that their way of achieving the goals they look to obtain can only be accomplished through terror.

I don't believe they are finished with us. I believe they want to catch us off guard again in another attack on U.S. soil. I thought a lot about our troops over in Pakistan and wondered what kind of Independence day they had. I just wish all these doubtful feelings I have could just go away. I want so desperately to go back to September 10th, 2001, and make it all go away. Unfortunately, I can't do that, nor can anyone else. I think of the strange things that I do to insure my safety now that would have been unimaginable ten months ago. When I travel to my office in Manhattan, I carefully scan the people that surround me on the train and gaze at their briefcases and bags for a signal to alert me to possible danger. I get on the Staten Island Ferry and reach under my seat to find out if there is a life preserver ready for use. I constantly peruse the waterways for approaching ships with containers and monitor the distance they keep from the ferry. As I walk from the ferry to my job I shiver as the helicopters take off from the downtown area. That sound still makes my heart pound. I stop at church many mornings and ask God to be there for me should there be another attack, as I will need his guidance. I believe that now he is aware of the evil, Satan-like people and is giving more attention to them. I kneel down and pray that maybe God can soften their hardened hearts if there is any heart left in them. I ask Him to be wherever my children and loved ones are so that they may escape any additional attacks. I want to see them grow old and have children and families of their own, the same wishes that I'm sure our ancestors wanted for all of us. I have personally come to accept the danger that lurks in the unknown. I know that at anytime, my life could be snatched away. I'm not afraid of death anymore. I am afraid of reliving the terror I felt on September 11th. I believe I must put my faith in God and that He knew the day I was born and the day he would prepare to bring me home. I just ask that he make it a bearable exit.

I want to know that the angels he sends to rescue me are choosing the younger souls over mine. These angels will be the ones who will best understand me since I have spent many years searching for the wings to fly high in the sky. After September 11th, I have a renewed outlook on life. I no longer search out happiness for me, I search out happiness for those I care for and for those that may never know the happiness I have already had. I wish for them the peace of love, the kind of love that comes with years of ups and downs, the searching deeply of our inner souls. I know that in my husband I discovered that kind of love. He was always the better person, the kinder one, the gentler one, the one who kept it together just with his genuine heart. No matter how hard I made it, he simplified it, no matter how difficult I became, he smiled. He was my strength, not in the sense of being big and strong, but in being the person I probably always wanted to be but lacked the courageous, self-denying attitude that he possesses. I look at my three sons, each with their own special qualities, and know that without the love of their father they probably would not have the hearts they possess.

I know that had my husband not been in my life during the past year, my recuperation from the World Trade Center trauma would have lasted longer. I have been told that he was patient and ran the house while I was medicated and totally incapable of making any decisions. I have done so much contemplating since September 11th that I realize now God had his plan right from the beginning. He took my parents when I was young, had me raised by the nuns and priests at Mount Loretto and gave me my husband to spend my life with. I am a true believer that the road is paved by Him, step by step, and although the road winds, curves, turns off and needs repairs, it is still the road we travel. Every once in a while the paving job God uses will lead to a road built to last. A road that he truly wants us to be on.

As we go on each day from here, it will be different. Although our values have changed, mostly for the better, we need to go forward without hesitation and believe that out of such a devastating trial can come triumph. I am speaking for those of us who were able to escape, not for those who died and their families. I cannot see—good coming out of the loss of life. As I sit here on the beach on the white sand continuing to listen to the laughter of the children, I smile and wish I could go back to those times. Watching the dads and moms helping with those sand castles, I wonder if they're actually helping to build the future of those children? I can still remember as a child those special times at the beach in Rockaway. My brother Jerry and I would attempt to build things in the sand. The only difference was, all we had then was a pail and shovel and a sand filter. Today the parents come with a truck load of different shapes and forms, shovels and even the flag to place on top of the finished product in hopes of creating a sand castle that will be remembered forever. These are the times that mold little souls into big hearts. The peace that comes with a child's laughter bouncing over the waves near the shore cannot be matched with any other sound.

These are the times I need in my life right now. Simple, honest and heartwarming, a sincere quiet and peace of mind. I know that I can't stay here forever just yet. Someday soon I hope to make this my permanent home. The summers are hectic with tourists, but from September through April, the tranquility of Ocean City, Maryland, is all I have ever dreamt of.

Here in this tranquility I can write down my thoughts and look to tomorrow without fear. There seems to be a safety net over me whenever I leave New York. I sleep better, think better, and I surely enjoy life better. Anxiety and fear have been known to alter personalities, damage relationships and even sometimes destroy them. Here in Maryland I find good in everything. I find smiles on the people I greet on my walks. The people here still fly flags and the marquee signs still read "God Bless America." Back in New York, people have gone back to honking the horns, yelling at each other, continued road rage and all that used to make New York, New York. For the few weeks after September 11th, everyone stood together, shared in tears, fears, love and renewal. Why can't it last? What truly makes one person happy? What is it that we want from life? Why can't we all band together heart to heart to let those evil people know that they have messed with the wrong country? The more they see us band together, the less likely they will believe they can pull us down with their evil ways. Yet, we seem to drift right back into the old pattern of treating our neighbors with disrespect. Well, I guess tomorrow is another day. I leave you with my thoughts of yesterday.

October 27, 2001

The Peace Of The Ocean

The ocean is mesmerizing, the waves a little rough
So much time has disappeared, enough is enough
Walking along under bright sunny skies
Gently pushing the hair away from my eyes

Now I see, not only the sun and the sea
I see far beyond as my life returns to me
As I bend and reach for a sand-filled shell
I look up at the man who brought me back from hell

I feel the breeze so refreshing so grand
It is not cold because someone's holding my hand
As we walk and plan for the future ahead
I think to myself I would marry him again

Out over the waves we see the dolphins swim free
That is what I want so much for this man and me,
As the seagulls fly by enjoying their flight
I'm thankful to God to once again see light

As couples pass we greet them hello
Our situation is something they will never know
Watching the fisherman with their poles and bait
It is like walking on the shore of heaven's gate

The peace, the tranquility, two lives intertwined
This could be my new home, I surely would not mind
For right here and now I have everything in sight,
Of all that is important for the rest of my life

The sun is going down and the people have dwindled
It is now time for us to once again mingle
As we stroll up the sand on this perfect beach
I know all my dreams are now within reach

Nearer we walk 'til we reach the dunes
As we turn one more time to glance at the moon
As I put my head on his shoulder and walked back home
This was a special time, we both know we're not alone

July 6, 2002

Tomorrow Is Another Day

I wake each morning knowing my time is only borrowed
None of us are guaranteed to wake again tomorrow
We go through the motions, we try desperately to believe
Someday we will walk again in this land of the brave and free
We follow where our faith will go, although we trust in God
Today I think we believe that heaven is not that far
The angels are flying, waiting for their chance to act
The fear that we are feeling is like the wind upon our back
We walk, we talk, we try to look, for the good in all the bad
Yet, we still are not smiling, we are too busy being sad
The terrorists are winning since we still live in fear
Some more than others can feel that they are near
Others seem to go about and live in their daily lives
Then there are the lonely widowers and depressed wives
The children of the firefighters, policemen and the lost
Who will pave our future and what will be the cost
End your day with peace and love, never forget to pray
For only then will you realize, tomorrow is another day!

Chapter Eighteen

Going Home

Now that I have supplied you with everything you need to know about me, where I came from, what I believe, I will now tell you where I'm going.

Believe it or not, I'm still fighting my company for Worker's Compensation and for unemployment benefits. I have been in and out of court since November. It is hard to imagine that anyone could be so cruel as to treat an employee, especially a dedicated employee, in this manner. The reason I have still been in court is because each time the hearing is set, my cowardly employers do not show. I told the judge, they can't face me, they can't bring themselves to accept the fact that they made a mistake. They fired me because they feared I would bring chaos and break down the other employees. They aren't even aware that the other employees were breaking me down that morning. I truly will never understand, except for the fact that they put off my bonuses until December. They claimed the first two quarters were not what they expected. I knew it was not true, because one of the employees who worked with the attorney and who did payroll always advised everyone when someone received additional monies. The attorneys themselves had recently taken a twenty-five-thousand-dollar bonus in May. I should have realized then that they were waiting for an opportunity to eliminate the idea of having to cover what they had promised. They saw an opportunity and unfortunately for me, unable to control my fears, they took advantage of it. The court had ordered that prior to the July 11th court hearing that the firm return to me my personal belongings. The day before, on July 10th, I was contacted to come and retrieve them. I contacted my brother who drove to New York and after work I headed back to Vesey Street for the first time since September 11th. I stayed on my cell phone as I walked along Broadway talking to my brother who was parked on Church and Vesey. The closer I got to Ground Zero the more I thought about the horror of that day. There before me was St. Paul's Church, still adorned with shirts, hats, signs and posters bidding farewell to all those lost that day. As I started down Vesey Street from Broadway, I immediately noticed that aside from the Stage Deli, all the businesses that once operated on the block were gone. Their doors closed, windows boarded, markings written on them with words of comfort to the many who died. What am I doing here? I asked myself. Were these belongings worth coming back here for? I phoned the contact person that the court had assigned to turn over my belongings. She answered the phone, I told her that I was down in the street and she said "I'm on my way down." As I stood looking at the devastation still before me, I turned to see my one boss, the one I had believed had cared for me during my employment, heading toward me. My attorneys strictly informed me to have no contact with any of my prior employers. As he approached me, I stood bewildered as he stretched out his arms to give me a hug. I stepped back immediately, wondering where this man's head was. Why would he attempt to greet me with a hug if I had been such a poor example for others? Why was there a big smile on his face as if we were two old friends reuniting? He then reached his hand to shake mine, and I found it so easy to pull away. I looked into the eyes of this man that I had respected for almost four years. I listened to his stories of success, went shopping for him and most importantly I treated his business as I treated my home, with care and protection. I even helped his employees on that unforgettable day ten months earlier. I looked straight in his eyes and asked, "Why did you do this to me?" He looked away and then said, "Business is business." He told me I looked well and when he realized there was no response left in my soul for him or his company, he turned and bid me farewell. As I watched him walk away, I wondered how he slept at night. How does he choose money over a person that cared so much? Was the money the real scenario? Or had my other boss become tired of my constant complaints about his seductive treatment of the young girls in the office? I continued to stare at his steps as he began to blend into the crowd and out of sight. I no longer could be hurt by these people. I knew in my heart I had moved on although I will never forget the victimization they put on me. I turned with a slight smile as I walked toward the car and exited Church and Vesey with the few personal items I had accumulated over the years. I knew it was over and I promised myself not to fall apart in court tomorrow. I would stand tall, I will be strong, I want to face them, I have waited ten months to do so.

My husband refused to let me go to court alone that day. He met me on the train and we headed down Bay Street hand in hand to face my friends turned enemies in front of the judge. My attorney, Mr. Bifulco, met me at the entrance and asked if I was ready. I told him that I was strong, and I won't fall apart as I had at the prior hearing. I just looked at him and said, "I have been honest since the beginning and I will continue to be honest." The judge will be able to see my sincerity and the devastation from not only my memories of September 11th, but also of the victimization of my employer.

I was totally shocked when the case was called. Once again, my employers did not appear. The judge did not hold back her anger as she laced into the insurance carrier attorney representing the company. The young woman's attorney simply stated that the company was no longer controverting the claim. The judge looked at her and agreed that the matter should finally be put to rest, exactly ten months later. The decision was in my favor, financially. I received compensation for the past ten months with approved medical payment. The case was adjourned until September in order to obtain the latest medical and psychological reports from my physicians.

I looked at the judge and thanked her, not for feeling the way she did but for believing that I had been telling the truth all along. I knew that at some point someone would believe in me, and see that there are companies that can deal an employee a dirty hand. I felt some satisfaction although I will always be cautious of trusting anyone in the near future. My sense of dedication had been altered indefinitely. As my husband and I walked back toward the train, he looked at me and said, "I knew you could do this, even when you wanted to give up. I believed you would do the right thing for us and for yourself. You won and hopefully those sons of ————, have learned a lesson." His anger toward my employer was overwhelming, even though he is so mildly mannered. It was hard for him to understand how they could have taken all the past ten months to such lengths to hurt me. I just smiled and said it is over, and that I need to start healing, to move on and not look back. I have been a survivor my whole life and I will get through this also. I thought about my family and decided you might want to read the poem I wrote them during their college graduations this year.

May 22, 2002

The Road To Success

This weekend brought happiness like I never knew
Three college degrees for my sons came true
One with a Master's, a Bachelor's and Associate's Degree
What more could a mom ask for in the land of the free

Now I ask where they go in the journey to tomorrow
Years of paying education with money earned and borrowed
Are they aware truly there are no more games to play
Because none of us are promised just one more day

I can only pray and give them my total praise
May they all find their dreams in the sunshine of their days
I never want them to know a day without shining
For our lives are bound, a bed of roses intertwining

May they walk on the path and breathe only fresh air
Knowing that their Dad and I will always be right there
Should they question whether they have true worth
I'll tell them to believe in heaven here on earth

Should they ever travel on the road in the wrong lane
The rainbow will lead them to safety in the rain
If they feel like going down their memories recalling
They'll know there's no chance of any of them falling

I wish you success, I wish you the best in your life
May you all find a woman like your brother's wife
Someone to share the days and bring you endless smiles
For we will be there always no matter the amount of miles

Our only request that we ask is to find room in your heart
For the man upstairs who helped to give you your start
If you truly want happiness then you will have to believe
That true happiness will come when you fall to your knees

Chapter Nineteen

The Final Chapter For Now

It is about eight a.m. on a Tuesday morning in August. Ironically as it seems, Tuesdays are grim reminders of all that has transpired during the past year. I'm sitting on the beach in Ocean City, Maryland, alone watching the fishermen and the seagulls. All seems so quiet, peaceful, I feel complete solitude and yet the nightmares continue. I still see planes heading in my direction. I'm always running in my dream, which probably explains why each morning I wake up tired. It was right here on the beach on October 25th when I rose from a drug-induced trance to realize that I still wanted to live. Why not? I worked hard to get to where I was and I loved my family. They waited a long time to see the healing begin and have their mother return to the land of the living. I can now speak easier about September 11th, but I will never accept or understand how our government fell asleep at the helm and left our lives totally in the hands of those firemen, policemen and innocent civilians who fought so desperately to save our lives. In return, so many of them, lost theirs.

I read the poems that I had written during my black-out period and realized how much pain I had truly been in. They are sad reminders of the world I sank into during that lost period of time. Whether the time period had been a day, a week, whatever, it was time that belonged to my life and those hateful terrorists took it from me.

August 11ᵗʰ, 2002

Eleven Months And Counting

God give me the strength that I desperately need this day
Knowing that in another month an anniversary comes our way
Not one that we can celebrate, not with balloons and a fancy cake
One that is very memorable, the day when many were taken away

Another sad reminder of the memories shared by all
Another day to remember how the towers once stood tall
When all the bells in all the cities ring out for all to hear
Stand up and shout this is our land, we no longer feel the fear

Light up all the harbors, let the lights shine into the skies
Remind all our people that eagles are still able to fly
Make us remember the lives we lost, the lost heroes unsung
Band us together, let the terrorists know they have not won

Ring the bells loud, put the lights all around our city
Remember the lost souls, for them we should feel pity
A cowardly act upon us, took their hearts away from here
The terrorists have no morals, their lifestyles will never compare

Open the gates to hell, take them down to where they belong
They don't deserve a trial, let the people decide right or wrong
Put them back in their corner, let them rot forever below
Give us back our dignity, let justice once again begin to flow

I wish I could remember my husband trying to take over the cooking and cleaning. That must have been a sight after thirty-two years of never entering the kitchen. I sadly do not remember being in this world when he had his heart attack and pacemaker surgery. He tells me, "You never left my side." I could not have been there because I can't remember any of it. I look at him now, how much I love him, how much I always did, but was afraid to really open myself up to him or my children. It all goes back to a childhood where everyone I loved, I lost. I was afraid to love, to grow close to anyone or anything. I suppose each one of us at some point in our lives have experienced this feeling of believing that it's easier not to love and lose than to love so much and lose someone forever. Since October, we talk more, laugh more and feel more, a lot more. My true friends are also a great part of my healing process. There were two who were at every crossroad to my healing. One of them just listened and shared my pain, tried to wipe away my tears and be there all the time. She has a great sense of humor and often reminds me of Lucille Ball. My other special friend prayed for me. Those prayers counted. My friend, Denise, and I went to high school together. Her relationship with God is solid, and whenever you ask her to pray for someone, the prayers are answered. She seems to have a special connection to the above. My relationship with God was always a priority, and yet now I have surrendered all of me to his care. *Que Sera Sera*—whatever will be will be. I didn't know at the time but now I believe that as long as I see His hands outstretched on my ascend, I will have nothing to fear during those last moments in this life. I can now accept the thought of death at anytime. I am ready! I wasn't on September 11th.

My brother was growing impatient with my behavior. Since our childhood he always knew me best and knew my good and bad qualities. He could not understand my fears. One day while we were speaking, he said, "Snap out of it already. I spent three years in Vietnam and I saw death. You have to put it out of your mind." I retorted, "You knew where you were going when you went to Vietnam, you knew you would be fighting, I simply went to work. There is no comparison. The terrorist attack on the World Trade Center was not supposed to happen here in New York. We should have never had known such fear and terror."

He also reminded me that for someone like me, who has such faith in God, knowing that death is imminent and that the bible tells us we will never know the day or time. We must all face and believe that death is probably the only ending that not one of us has any control over.

My new job will begin next week and my twelve-year profession of being a paralegal is about to come to a close. I think of it as twelve years of building knowledge and now I have chosen to walk away. I know in my heart that when you pray for guidance and an opportunity appears, it is your obligation to take it. If we pray for something and the answer appears, yet we choose to ignore it, what was the sense of praying? Maybe at the time it does not warrant consideration, then choosing a restaurant for dinner or a movie to see warrants as little. So I will be working across the street from my home in Staten Island, New York. I will be the coordinator for an after-school program at Our Lady Star of the Sea School. I gave little thought to accept the job and of course I put no monetary value on the decision. After all, money won't bring you happiness and sometimes seeking it out can truly be the root of all evil. The same evil I found on that bright September morning a year ago.

The company that I'm leaving in New York gave me a memorable farewell. My one boss, Bill Gallagher, said, "I won't stand in the way of the Lord, I'm no fool. If he wants you, then I wish you all the best." He told me that the door will always remain opened should I decide to return. I promised to keep in touch and I will because without their understanding and patience I would not have survived the return to the city. I wish I could have worked for them four years ago. It would have eased my anxiety a lot sooner because I would not have seen so many die. I knew I had to return to the city and immediately a door opened not only to employment but to true humanity and understanding. My other boss, Lou Martine, knew how to heal an injured soul. God bless you all at McMahon, Martine and Gallagher, it was an honor to have been a part of your staff. Your employees are lucky to have you in their corner. As I mentioned above, money isn't everything. The day after I left, I wrote this poem to them:

August 8, 2002

McMahon Martine and Gallagher

Today I parted ways with the company that stood by my side
I felt so many emotions, the tears just filled my eyes
I said goodbye to new friends, I asked them to pray for me
As I continue in this walk, a walk that will set me free

The doctors said in no short terms, that near home I should be
Knowing that the next best place is Our Lady Star of the Sea
I'll be near to God and him to me, will the fears ever fade
Did I do the right thing leaving, or should I have tried to stay?

I stood and said goodbye as the ferry pulled from the dock
What am I doing? Is my mind still suffering from shock?
I watched the buildings shrinking, I saw that gapping hole
How I miss those towers, will the memories ever grow old

I thought about the battle, have the terrorists captured my heart
I fought back the tears and listened to the engines begin to start
The bright lights of New York, the peace of the early morn
Now I just listen to the planes that above me constantly soar

The skyline is so peaceful as the boat crosses through the bay
I look at this beautiful city, knowing the pain will never go away
Someday New York I'll return to the buildings standing tall
Whenever my fears of September 11th no longer make me crawl

So long to my new friends, to Grace and all the crew
You stood along side of me, even when you all knew
That I was scared and frightened but you helped to see me through
Goodbye to a great company, I will never forget friends so true

To Lou, Bill, Tony and Mike, my thanks I give to you all,
Anytime you need me, don't hesitate, just give me a call
You were right there for me with your kindness and concern
This is surely one bridge my heart will refuse to burn

When I think about the company that I had worked for during September 11th, I try to overcome my animosity toward them. I will always think twice before ever trusting a company again with my future. I had believed I would have worked for that company until my retirement. I only wonder how they justify victimizing me a second time within three weeks of our nation's tragedy. The good news is I have won both my Workmen's Compensation case and my unemployment insurance because my former employers were foolish enough not to show up for any of the hearings. I knew in my heart they would have a hard time lying to my face. Cruelty always comes back to haunt people. I don't wish it on them but I believe that no one will ever care for their company the way I did. I had no real friends for as the saying goes, "Leadership is lonely." Since I was their office manager along with being the only paralegal, I kept to myself, and I kept all of their secrets. My loyalty was always one of my greatest qualities. If I told each of them the depth of contempt each has for the other, the business would surely collapse as easily as the towers.

The time has been passing slowly as I sit here along the shore. The waves are sounding more like a running stream. The fishermen have left after their early morning catch and the seagulls are waiting in anticipation for the snacks to be opened on the blankets. The sounds of laughter echo from the water, children frolicking, enjoying the beautiful day at the beach. Lovers are walking along hand in hand and I can hear in the distance the parents yelling out their children's names to come in from the water. Photographs are being snapped and memories stored for the summer album of 2002, smiles you never want to forget. Those were also happy times for our family, oh so many years ago. Those were the good old days. Our lives are so different now, it is a treat to have everyone together for just one more day at the beach, one more family photo, one more day of bonding and sharing. I have finally come to the realization that you have to let go, it was very hard for me to do since noone ever let go of me. Now I have a married son, a loving daughter-in-law, both teachers, my middle son is living and working in northern Maryland and my baby is preparing to take the New York City Firemen's test in November and is currently a full-time college student in his third year. It was like yesterday when I sat here watching them play in the water. Where has all the time gone? My oldest was four years old when we first came to Ocean City. The formative years are over for them, they are who they are, the roads that they choose will be their roads, and their morals and values must be accounted for by them and them alone. I look attentively at these young parents and wonder if they truly know the joy of watching children grow, the pains of letting kids soar free and the unconditional love that will cause me to worry about each of mine forever. It was difficult enough in safe harbors. With the changing times, I suppose most of us just look at tomorrow instead of looking to the future. Sadly enough, many are still looking back and probably will for months, even years to come.

The people who were seating in front of me are now scrabbling to retrieve their wet blankets as the tide begins to rise. A seagull just lifted a bag of chips from an unattended blanket. Great idea for a Wise potato chip commercial. The lifeguards are blowing their whistles to alert swimmers of a riptide in effect. It is one of God's greatest creations to listen to, the ocean's roar and then the calm as the waves come in and out. The laughter of the children now begins to become whines as their bodies tire from the constant running in or through the waves. The jet boats are out and the schools of dolphins are heading south to the inlet. So many wonders about this creation but like everything else in life we should never let our guard down. Whether against the ocean's power or against evil terrorists who are lurking in the shadows so adamantly trying to take all these precious joys away from us.

The sun is now beating down and I can feel the heat against my body. I guess today will be the first time this year that I venture into the water. I took my lavender tube, my life raft as I call it, and walked into the ocean. It took sometime to pass over the breaking of the waves. Once beyond them, I situated myself comfortably across the tube, and for the first time in a year, I began to look at life in a brighter way. Here I was gazing out onto the amazing Atlantic Ocean. The boats were going by, and in a distance, a container ship headed north probably to New York or Wilmington, Delaware. I looked up at the heavens, then out toward the horizons and once in awhile I waved intermittently at my husband who stood guard at the shoreline. I floated around and many thoughts came to me during that hour of complete solitude. I thought back over the last eleven months. I thought back to times when I felt I would never return to a normal state of mind. Don't misinterpret my sense of the word "normal," since normal only existed prior to September 11th. Nothing will ever be normal in that sense again. I did admit to myself I had come a long way. After I stopped taking the medication, Xanax, I started to get my thinking cap back on. I started to remember more intense details of the many things I had witnessed on that horrific day. As a wave breaking close to me almost caught me in its wrath, I protected myself by moving quickly toward it. I guess that sums up the past months of my life. Each time another force reached toward me to bring me down, I pushed past it. I survived an ordeal that many could never comprehend. While resuming my relaxing, floating position, I thought about how much I cared for my family and friends, even those who were not there when I needed them. I looked up and prayed this prayer: Dear God; let me continue to walk in your grace, honor your beliefs and be there for anyone who knocks at my door. For I have been in the position of need over the last year and I know how much I welcomed all the opened doors. Forgive those who put money before human emotion. Bless all the people who opened their hearts and minds to my situation. Please watch over Ginger and Al, Craig and his family and all those who lost loved ones on September 11th. Their losses will never be understood or accepted by them or me. Some feelings can never change no matter how hard we try. Grant them the guidance to take one step closer to you each day and a step further away from the horror of September 11th. Help us all to believe that our government will try harder in the future to protect the people of the United States. Most of all dear Lord, keep us safe whether we believe in your powers or not, whether we put our trust in you or not, bless the people, black, white, Asian and yes even those people who look to destroy. Bless and protect the children who look forward to a life as you prepared it. Take the nonbeliever, make him believe, the weak, make strong, the sad, make happy and give to the frightened your everlasting presence.

As I look up toward the shore, I can see my husband waving frantically as I had drifted quite a distance out. By now, the lifeguard was signaling me to come back in and, although where I was seemed so peaceful and safe, I turned and headed toward shore. My husband asked, "What were you doing out there so long?" I responded by saying, "I was talking to a friend. I was quite safe and you should not have been so upset."

I don't believe that we have seen the end of the terrorists' attacks. Unfortunately, many of you would like to think we have. It is sad to think that all the beauty God gave us to enjoy can be snatched away in seconds. Our children, our parents, our family, how does one ever get past that kind of pain? I think of our country, and I still have the American flags on my cars, on both of my homes, but especially in my heart. I'm proud to be an American, I'm proud that I can live free once again, though maybe only in my heart, but as long as I can walk a good walk alongside my God and know when my time comes I will be prepared. I will be the first to tell him to please take care of the children, take care of the parents of those children, give them the joy I knew for the past twenty-eight years, let them play in the ocean, walk the shores, pick the shells, and when back in the big cities, help them to walk with their heads held high, and never forget that this is our country, that there is a God, and forever more may we all be blessed with safety. God Bless America. I leave you with the final poem for now.

August 19, 2002

My Road Back Continues

My book is now complete, the poems are ready to be read
I am giving you the best of me, it comes from my heart and head
I don't expect that everyone will see things as I do
But just try to imagine what so many people went through

The road was long and rocky, but I followed it anyway
Knowing full heartedly the end of the road comes someday
It is only a fork for me to decide, which turn I need to take
As long as I can continue to heal, a complete recovery I'll make

I pity those who hurt me, things worked out in my favor
Your turn will come when you will answer to, only our creator
Maybe he'll forgive you because everyone deserves a chance
Then the angels will rescue you and we all again shall dance

For all my family and friends, bless you for all you did
You treated me so kindly, your hearts so willing to give
I will always be grateful for the prayers, cards and love
You shall receive your reward from our God who sits above

Should you be sad and lonely, I promise to be there for you
Sometimes it takes real strength for others to bring you through
I leave you now with memories, so many words left unsaid
Love will take the pain from your heart, but please don't ever forget.

About the Author

Joann Namorato is making her writing debut in this feature story into her life and the events of September 11, 2001. She was born on November 20, 1950 in the South Bronx of New York City. After having to deal with many unfortunate deaths in her family, both she and her brother were placed in Mount Loretto, an orphanage for young children. She recalls mostly fond memories of the "Mount," as it is commonly referred and stills keeps in contact with many of the people who touched her life there. In fact, it was there where she met her eventual husband of thirty-two years. Joann and her husband Patrick continue to reside in Staten Island, the birthplace of their three children, Brian, Daniel and Keith.

Mrs. Namorato's heart goes out to all those families who were brought to their knees by the horrific events of September 11th. Although there are very few words to express your pain, just believe that your loved ones are watching over us every minute of every day. The author concludes with a line from a Gospel psalm: "And he will raise you up on eagles wings, bear you on the breath of dawn and make you to shine like the sun, and hold you, hold you in the palm of his hand."

0-595-24676-1